Toddler's First Steps

A **"Best Chance" Guide** to Parenting Your Six-Month- to Three-Year-Old

FIRST EDITION

First published in Canada in 2002 by
Macmillan Canada, an imprint of CDG Books Canada

National Library of Canada Cataloguing in Publication Data

Toddler's first steps : a best chance guide to parenting your six-month- to three-year-old

Includes index.
ISBN 1-55335-018-9

1. Toddlers. 2. Parenting. 3. Child rearing.
I. British Columbia. Ministry of Health Planning.

HQ774.5.T62 2002   649'.122   C2002-900344-X

1 2 3 4 5 TRANS 06 05 04 03 02

This book is available at special discounts for bulk purchases by your group or organization for sales, promotions, premiums, fundraising and seminars. For details, contact: Government Publication Services at 1 800 663-6105 web site www.publications.gov.bc.ca

The following photos reprinted with permission from Health Canada. Photos on pages 110 and 114 are from Active Living, Health Canada 2002. Photos on pages 3, 16, 33, 37, 40, and 87 are from Children/Daycare, Health Canada 2002. Photos on pages 15, 41, 52, 66, 73, and 84 are from Children/Youth, Health Canada 2002. Photos on pages 28, 39, 53, 55, 68, 69, 71, 75, 81, 83, 88, 108, 110, 111, 112, 113, and 117 are from Family, Health Canada 2002. Photos on pages 114, 115 and 116 are from Healthy Images, Health Canada 2002. All Health Canada photos are copyright Minister of Public Works and Government Services Canada, 2002.

Photo on page 60 is by Jean Konda-Witte; reprinted with permission.

Illustrations on pages 14 and 57 by Dave Mazierski. Illustrations on pages 56, 97, 101, 102, and 103 by Crowle Art Group.

Printed by the Queen's Printer of British Columbia, Canada

Contents

Preface

Toddler's First Steps is part of an information series on early childhood development that began with *Baby's Best Chance: A Best Chance Guide to Pregnancy, Parenthood and Infant Care*. *Toddler's First Steps* is intended to assist parents and caregivers of children six months to three years of age in understanding what contributes to their child's healthy growth and development. It will also help parents and caregivers provide the environment and support that contributes to that growth and development. *Toddler's* is packed with important information and safety tips that parents and caregivers will want and need as they nurture and support these young children.

Appreciation is extended to the many professionals within the Ministry of Health Planning and the Ministry of Children and Family Development who were involved in the selection of topics and the review of the text for this handbook. We would also like to thank a number of other Ministries who contributed to the information in this book and the public health staff in Health Authorities for their contribution and review.

Thanks are extended to the following individuals for their contributions to this handbook:
Joanne Bergman, Loss Prevention Co-ordinator, Vehicle Safety Strategies, ICBC
Meng Cheng, Product Safety Officer, Health Canada
Linda Christensen, Manager, Vehicle Safety Strategies, ICBC
Lynn Guest, Dental Coordinator, Fraser Health Authority

Elizabeth Heinz, Manager, Provincial Programs Loss Prevention Services, ICBC
Meg Hickling, Sexual Health Educator
Linda McDonnell and Early Childhood Educator colleagues, Vancouver Island
Marnie Moore, Public Health Nurse & Certified Lactation Consultant, Vancouver Island Health Authority
Karen Pielak, Nurse Epidemiologist, Epidemiology Services, BC Centre for Disease Control
Ian Pike and Deanne Udy, The Red Cross
Kerry O'Donohue, Pacific Post Partum Support Society
Vision Advisory Committee of BC

We would also like to thank the staff from the agencies endorsing this publication for their review and input on content.

When you see

 there will be a quick fact marked "Did You Know?"

 there will be important child safety information

Introduction By Dr. Clyde Hertzman

Director, Human Early Learning
Partnership of British Columbia

"The first years last forever" is much more than a slogan. Research conducted in Canada and around the world clearly shows that our health, well-being, and coping skills in adulthood and old age are strongly influenced by our start in life. All stages in life are significant, but the period from conception to school age is especially important. During this time the brain develops with amazing rapidity, organizing and reorganizing in response to the child's environment. By the time of school entry, the intellectual, social, and emotional development of the child will have been fundamentally shaped by this process and, in turn, will influence the child's future life chances. In Canada, large differences in development exist among children by the time they enter school. Approximately one quarter of Canadian children enter school requiring further developmental support. The sad fact is that this is largely preventable.

A full range of stimuli affects the newborn: visual, verbal, emotional, physical, touch, smell, and taste. Children who grow up in stimulating environments have the best chance for a good start in life. We now know a lot about the kinds of early surroundings that work best. We know that children need a responsive and interactive environment of talking and reading, mentoring and encouragement of exploration through play, warmth and acceptance, and protection from teasing and punishment.

Effective parenting means creating environments for children that have these characteristics. Family stability, close and supportive relationships, and a sense of personal security are protective factors in the lives of children. But parents cannot do it all alone. Economic security and workplace flexibility are essential supports for parents. Neighbourhoods that are safe and caring of children; and the quality, accessibility, and affordability of child care and development programs make a big difference too. The results from effective early childhood stimulation and support programs show that they have positive paybacks, and that these can endure for a lifetime.

It is with these thoughts in mind that this book has been developed. The intention is to provide parents of young children ages six months to three years with practical information on how to best support, encourage, and help their children to grow and develop to their full potential.

CHAPTER 1

Development: The Early Years Are Important

You may have heard the expression "the first years last forever." This means that the experiences your child has in the early months and years of life help shape his brain's structure, organization, and function for the rest of his life. At birth your child's brain is not fully developed. As your child explores the world his brain acts like a sponge, absorbing events, experiences, and feelings as it develops. You feed your child healthy food and provide active play so that his body can grow and thrive. You also need to provide positive emotional, physical, and intellectual experiences so his brain can grow and be healthy. During your child's first three years, nerve cells in the brain grow and connect to form systems that control things like moving, thinking, remembering, and expressing emotions. Most of these systems are formed as children interact with their parents, caregivers, or other people or objects. When children have experiences over and over again, these nerve systems become permanent and shape the way they think and behave. A child who is provided with love and stimulation in the early years has the best chance for these organizational brain connections to develop in healthy ways.

The most important ingredient in making sure your child has every chance to grow a strong, resourceful brain is a secure, loving relationship with you and others around him. This means:

- Interacting with your child as much as you can by talking, playing, singing, or reading.
- Lots of holding and cuddling. (This causes the child's brain to release hormones that he needs to grow.)

- Responding to your child's signals and cues—including sounds, movements, facial expressions, and the way he makes or avoids eye contact. This helps him learn not only how to communicate but also that his needs and feelings are important.
- Praising and encouraging your child, which helps him learn about being understood.
- Establishing regular routines and rituals.
- Creating a safe environment for exploring.
- Choosing quality child care, both short term (babysitting) and long term (daycare).
- Being very selective about what your child watches on TV.
- Finding opportunities to teach behaviours that work well with groups of children and adults.

How Your Child's Personality Grows

Your child's personality develops in much the same way as her body grows: new skills come after practising the ones your child already knows well. The first and most important building block in the development of a healthy personality is the *learning of trust*. The beginning of this learning is thought to happen in the first year of life. The sense of trust can of course be increased or decreased after that time, but the foundation is developed during the first 12 months. In order to establish a healthy trust, your child needs consistent, loving care from a nurturing person. This person does not need to be an actual parent, but a person or group who responds to the child in a loving and caring way. Young children are best supported when a network of caring people forms around them. Your child learns trust by having her basic needs (such as for food and comfort) tended to quickly and in a caring way. If you react to a hungry cry by always or almost always providing enough food in a calm and caring way your child will learn to trust you. When you respond to your child's cry you are showing her that you will come back after being away. If you consistently speak to your child in a harsh tone, don't have any predictable routines, don't respond to your child's needs, and have frequent and sudden changes in your home, your child may begin to mistrust you and others. If this basic trust is not established, future stages may be delayed or difficult to reach for your child.

Help develop your child's sense of trust by:
- Responding to her needs in a loving way.
- Holding, cuddling, and showing her interesting toys or games.
- Feeding her enough of the right foods when hungry (e.g., warm milk).

All families have times of change and tension, and parents have different levels of skills in child care. You won't cause damage to your child's personality forever by not being a perfect parent all the time. Letting your child cry for short periods when settling down for the night, for example, won't hinder her development of trust. The development of trust takes time. Trust will develop over a period of time as your child learns to rely on you to satisfy her basic need for things such as food, warmth, and caring.

The second stage in the development of a child's personality usually occurs between one and three years of age. This stage is known as **autonomy versus shame and doubt** (or **independence versus dependence**). Your child learns that he can control himself, his body, and others around him. He takes delight in knowing new skills and loves doing things for himself, including making decisions and choices. The shame and doubt come into play only if your child is made to feel unimportant or self-conscious when his attempts to do things fail or result in disasters. He also needs to do things for himself that he can control, such as getting dressed, feeding himself, or washing. When this stage is reached you will notice increased willpower and self-control in your toddler.

Help your toddler develop independence by:
- Encouraging him in his attempts to do things even if he fails.
- Checking that shame or ridicule are not a part of your home.
- Letting him do whatever it is he can, such as dressing or washing, and praising him for it.
- Encouraging him to try new activities at which he has a good chance of succeeding, such as throwing a ball or doing a somersault.
- Not pushing your child too hard to perform new skills once he has shown you he can do something easier. Let him have a sense of being able to do each new skill really well.

Learning About Your Child

Temperament is a person's distinct nature or character; it is "who we are." Some children's temperaments are obvious right from birth, while others will show over time. If you have more than one child, you will already have first-hand experience of temperament. One child may be very shy while another may be outgoing; one may be athletic and another a bookworm. Your home environment and who your child spends time with will have some effect on her temperament, but it is mostly just an inborn part of the kind of person she is. Your job is to find ways to support your child.

Your traits and temperament will not necessarily be the same as your child's. If you're active and outgoing, it may be harder for you to understand a child who's quiet and shy. If you love to spend time alone, it may be challenging to meet the needs of a toddler who always wants to play with you or other children. Learning to accept and work with your child's temperament rather than trying to change it will make both your lives easier and more pleasant. Your child's temperament may be seen in a number of ways, such as activity level, how predictable she is, how she reacts to new situations, and how adaptable she is. Does she react intensely or mildly to events? Is she easily distracted or can she focus well? What's her attention span like? How is her general mood?

What You Can Do to Support Your Child's Temperament

Try this exercise: If you are right-handed, take a pen in your left hand, and if you are left-handed, take the pen in your right. Now write your name and address. How did that feel? Difficult, uncomfortable, slow, unnatural, that you are not doing as good a job as you know you could? Now imagine trying to live your life that way. Forcing your child to be someone she's not is just as difficult for her as this writing exercise was for you. She may, with practice, eventually be able to act in a certain way, but this won't be easy or feel natural to her.

The key is to acknowledge and support your child's temperament. It's also important to teach her the skills that require learning and experience, such as kindness, an appreciation of learning, tolerance, and decision making.

Ways to Understand Temperament

- Understand that your child's temperament is not a choice, but rather how she naturally feels about things.
- Try not to label your child's temperament, and certainly not when she can hear you. A child who grows up with the belief that she is shy or not good in sports will tend to live up to those expectations.
- Be prepared to readjust your expectations of what you may have thought your child would be like. Boys are not always rough and tumble and not all girls like to play with dolls. Let your child lead you to discover her talents and preferences.

Ways to Help Your Child Work with Her Temperament

Find ways to help your child direct her tendencies into positive activities. This will make her more comfortable, and will help her to learn ways of working with her temperament. (See "Help Your Child Behave," page 72.)

- If your child is shy or slow to warm up, instead of forcing her to say hello and goodbye, encourage her to wave to people. After she waves, compliment her on how polite she was and how perhaps next time she could say bye-bye. She is learning polite behaviour and is interacting with people to the extent of her comfort level. A child who tends to be shy or slow to warm up may take longer to get used to a new play group. You can help by letting your child sit with you and observe until she's ready to join in. Supporting your child's temperament does not mean that she can do whatever she wants. Not joining the play group is not an option, and neither is ignoring family and friends. But allowing her to join in at a slower rate or to play in a different manner is simply helping her to develop skills she will need.

- If your child is very energetic, provide opportunities for her to move around as much as possible and to safely explore the world using her body. She may excel in sports, dance, or just simply running around the backyard for an hour. If she must be still for a period of time, give her something to do with her hands, such as playdough, or have her turn pages in a book or push a toy on her lap. Play games that give your child the opportunity to move and let her help you around the house with chores and other tasks.

- If your child tends to be easily frightened, talk to him about his fears. Even if they seem silly to you, realize that they are very real to him. Together think of ways to overcome fears, such

as checking the closet together for monsters or holding your child on your lap when near a dog. Let him know that you believe he can learn to cope with his fears: *"Someday I bet you could be friends with that dog if we visit him often and get to know him."*

- If your child is sensitive, he may be uncomfortable with bright lights and loud noises. Try to dim the lights and reduce noise from the radio or television. If tags in his clothing or wrinkles in his socks bother him, try to adjust his clothing so that he can tolerate it. Ignoring requests for clothing to be adjusted or noise to be decreased won't cure your child of his sensitivities. He will only continue to be distracted by the discomfort and be unable to focus well on other tasks.

- If your child reacts intensely to new situations, try breaking new things down into simple, small steps, such as *"This is how you sit on your bike, this is where your feet go, and this is where your hands go"* instead of *"Jump on and let's ride."* Simplify your life—don't take your child to places that require behaviour such as being quiet or sitting for a long time. Restaurants and shopping malls may be too difficult for an enthusiastic child at this age. Give adequate warning before any change, such as leaving the park or bedtime, and praise your child when he deals well with difficult situations.

How Your Child Grows Physically

Your child will generally develop his physical abilities in a step-by-step way. He will start with simple activities before going on to more difficult ones, such as grasping with his fist before using his fingers and thumb. His speech will also start simply, with cooing, crying, and squeals, and gradually move on to specific sounds and then words. Although the pattern of physical development is fairly predictable, every child will pass through these stages at different rates. Some will walk at nine months, others at 14 months. They are still following the same pattern, just at different times.

You will also notice that your child's ability to do things is developing in two more directions: from his head to his toes and from large movements to smaller ones. Your child will have control of his upper body before his legs and feet. He will lift his head first, then his chest, and soon he'll be rolling and then sitting. Movements involving the lower part of his body—like crawling, standing, and walking—happen later. He will have control of his hands before his feet, and will sit before he can stand. Larger movements such as rolling over and kicking happen before fine movements such as finger and thumb control.

The toddler years are a time of great change and growth. Your child goes from not moving much as a baby to a running, talking, exploring little person. Children typically triple their birth weight and increase their height by 50% in the first year of life. If they kept up this amazing rate of growth, they would be nearly 725 kg (1600 pounds) and over 3.6 metres (12 feet) tall at five years of age!

Watching these changes in your child can be fascinating. One day he'll slap at a dangling toy, and soon he'll be able to grab it, even if he is a bit clumsy. By the time he's nearly a year old, he'll learn to pick up smaller objects. As he gets older, he'll start to do more complicated things like stacking blocks, fitting objects together and, later, doing simple puzzles. These are all examples of what to expect.

There are many reasons why your child may be a little slower or quicker to reach physical growth milestones. Family traits have a very strong effect on height, weight, and rate of growth. If your child is ill for an extended period of time, he may grow a little more slowly or show skills a little later than other children of the same age. A very important factor in your child's growth—good nutrition—is one that you can control. So be sure to provide the best food you can to fuel your child's rapid growth in his toddler years. Nurturing has also been found to have an effect on how well your child develops. Talk or sing, hug, cuddle, comfort, love, and care for him as much as possible. For information on what your child may be able to do at certain stages, see pages 20 to 39. For information on feeding your toddler, see Chapter 2.

Is Crawling a Lost Art?

Crawling or creeping, a developmental skill that was expected to occur at about six to eight months of age, is no longer an activity for a number of children. Now some children will go from lying to sitting to walking, without crawling at all. This may be because of the "Back to Sleep" program, which encourages us to lie babies on their backs for sleep in order to decrease the likelihood of Sudden Infant Death Syndrome (SIDS). Always sleeping on her back may have changed how your child needs to move about to see the world. "Tummy time"—with parents or caregivers close by, observing and interacting—becomes even more important. When on her tummy, a child pushes up with her arms and raises her head in order to see around her. This raising of the head leads to kicking, arm movements, and eventually to crawling. It is a play activity that is needed for muscle development and to allow the head shape to develop as it should. It will also help the neck to become strong.

Laying your child on her back to sleep is very important. When she is awake, spend some time each day playing with her while she's on her tummy. This awake tummy time will encourage her to use her arms to raise her head and look around, and will help her to develop strength in her upper body.

The Child Born Early, or Smaller Than Expected

Your premature baby will usually catch up to other children by about the end of the first year of life. The old formula is to "adjust the age," meaning that if your child was born two months early, take two months off her real age to see what you might be expecting her to do at certain ages. This "adjusted age" is usually not used after about one and a half years of age. If your child had a very low birth weight (less than about 1 kilogram or 2 pounds), she may continue to be behind other children of the same age group well into the toddler and preschool years. Extra attention and encouragement can help these children catch up in their development. Hearing testing is important for premature or smaller-than-expected children, since there is an increased risk of a hearing impairment if your child's birth weight was less than 1.5 kilograms or about 3 pounds.

The premature or small-for-gestational-age child may also need to continue nighttime feeding for longer than an average-sized infant does. If you have concerns about your child's weight or frequency of feedings, talk to your doctor or public health nurse.

If You're Concerned About Your Child's Development

You have probably discovered that your child is unique, and will meet, exceed, or lag behind in various skills. Just as you may be skilled at fine handiwork and your partner may be all thumbs, so will your child have skills that differ from other children in his age group. The key is to watch for progress in abilities and development. Your child might be one, two, or more months behind on rolling over or walking compared with the other children you see, but the important thing is that he's trying to do more now than he did last month. Is he pulling himself up when weeks ago he was happy to sit or lie? Is he pointing at objects that he wants? Remember the patterns described above in "How Your Child Grows Physically." Is your child basically following these patterns?

As a parent you may be worried about whether your child is developing normally. This is a typical part of caring for your child. Try not to worry too much, but at the same time don't ignore your instincts. If something is telling you there's a problem, talk to your doctor or public health nurse. Early recognition is very important in helping children with special needs learn how to work with their strengths and to develop basic skills that may be harder for them to achieve.

Helping Your Child Sleep

The main point to remember about sleep is that both you and your child need enough sleep in order to function well during the day. Whatever you may be doing in order to get enough sleep is most likely right for you. You may be sharing your bed, also known as co-sleeping, or you may have your child in a crib, bed, or even sleeping on the floor in your room. Make sure your child is safe and happy with any arrangements. Make sure that your child is secure and that the surface he's sleeping on is safe for him—waterbeds are not safe for a young child. Also, if you are co-sleeping with your child, do not drink alcohol or take drugs. This is not safe for a child. Be sure that the way you normally sleep allows you to wake easily and that you are a peaceful sleeper. See page 102 for more information on cribs and beds.

If your toddler is having difficulty either getting to sleep or staying asleep, it may not seem as though

it's his problem so much as *your* problem. A toddler may be merely cranky or in need of an extra nap, but you on the other hand may have to go to work, or look after a tired child all day after not having enough sleep. It does not take long for a toddler's sleep problem, and hence a parent's sleep problem, to become very difficult for a parent to cope with. It can influence how you feel about your child. If you are constantly tired and feeling miserable because your child wakes you, it's hard not to begin feeling resentment and anger toward him. Your normal patience level may be lowered due to fatigue as well.

It may seem as though the sleepless nights will never end, but be assured that sleep problems in toddlers are very common and can usually be managed or even cured. Getting enough rest at night isn't just a matter of being lucky enough to have a child who is a "good sleeper." Parents can influence their children's sleep patterns by developing regular bedtime routines and habits. If your child is having sleep problems, it isn't too late to take steps to meet this challenge; however, a plan and patience is needed.

> As good sleep habits develop, you may notice that your child is better able to learn new skills. He will also be less irritable, happier, and better able to control himself.

How Much Sleep Does a Toddler Need?

Every child will need a different amount of sleep to be happy, but usually you can expect that:

- At six months, your child may sleep about 11 to 12 hours at night and have two naps, usually one in the morning and one in the afternoon, each lasting one to two hours.
- By one year most children sleep about a total of 14 hours a day. They may still have a nap in the morning and afternoon.
- By age two your toddler will probably be sleeping 11 to 12 hours at night and have a one- to two-hour nap in the afternoon.
- By age three your toddler will most likely be sleeping about 12 hours at night, and may have a short nap or may have stopped napping altogether. Some children will continue to have afternoon naps until five years of age.

> Generally, if your child is not sleeping through the night by six months of age, you may want to examine her bedtime routines to see if some changes will help her to sleep better. Remember that you are not alone in dealing with sleep problems—this is a common challenge for many parents. You can talk with your doctor, public health nurse, or other parents. There are also many books available on sleep issues and children.

Developing Bedtime Routines

Every family will have different routines related to bedtime. For some it's brushing their child's teeth and a story, for others it's talk and prayers, and for some it's rocking until the child is asleep. You can take some steps now to establish bedtime routines that will help your child form good sleep patterns and habits. Remember that sleep habits are learned, so be patient and work on developing a routine.

Try to make bedtime a pleasant time of the day that your toddler looks forward to. You can do this by spending time with her doing something that is quiet and enjoyable for both of you. If possible, set a routine and stick to it. This way she will know what to expect, when, and for how long. If you always brush her teeth, cuddle, and read her three stories, then she will know that this is the plan and won't be tempted to try to get "just one more," which delays her bedtime. It's a good idea to tell your child when there's "one more book to go" or "three more pages and then bedtime" so that she knows what's coming and is better able to go along with your plan.

Hints to Help Establish a Peaceful Bedtime

- Give your child some time to unwind after her day. It's hard to go from running and playing to sleeping, so try to slow her down by involving her in quiet activities, such as a bath or reading a story.
- If there's a lot of activity in your house at bedtime, a child may be too excited to sleep and want to stay up with the family. Although it may not always be possible, the rest of the family could either have some quiet time or at least be away from the bedroom.
- Try to make bedtime a special time, when your child can talk with you about events in her day. With a toddler it may be you who does most of the talking, but developing this habit will serve you well in later years. Your child will come to know that this is the time of day when she has your full attention, when you are both relaxed and she can share with you in a quiet and close way.
- Give your child some choices at bedtime. For example, let her choose what story to read, which pyjamas to wear, or which toy to take to bed.

- Let your child have bedtime rituals. Putting particular toys in the bed, holding a special blanket, choosing a story, or closing the closet door can all be important to a child's sense of security.
- If your child seems to be having trouble settling down to sleep and is staying awake long after being put in bed, look at when and how much she sleeps during the day. Sleeping late in the day or taking long naps may be taking the place of nighttime hours of sleep. You may need to gradually shorten daytime naps or gradually move the time of the nap to earlier in the day so that your child will be tired at bedtime.
- Watching television, even if you are sitting with your child, won't give her the chance to unwind and have close personal time with you. Watching television may only serve to stimulate or scare a child if the shows are active or violent.
- When your child was younger, you may have rocked her to sleep and gotten up during the night to feed and then rocked her to sleep again. As your child gets older, help her learn to fall asleep on her own so that when she wakes during the night she will know how to settle herself to sleep again. There are many ways to do this. Some parents gradually put their child down a little sooner—first before she's sound asleep, and then before her eyes are shutting. Eventually they get to the point where they can put their child down while she's awake but relaxed. Other parents will let their child cry, checking on her regularly until she falls asleep.
- If your child is afraid of the dark, or is just more comfortable with some light, plug in a nightlight or leave the door open and turn on a light outside her room.

▶ **Q: "My one-year-old is still waking up for a feed and cuddle at two in the morning, and I'm exhausted. What should I do?"**

▶ **A:** Sleep researchers tell us that we never really sleep through the night. We wake up from time to time, and put ourselves back to sleep without remembering the waking. This is a skill that babies and toddlers learn over time. Children are quick to develop habits, both good and bad. Waking to feed at night may have become a pattern for your child.

She's not really hungry, just very used to this routine. Your fatigue may mean that it's time to develop new patterns so that both you and your child get enough sleep.

There are as many ways to deal with night wakings as there are tired parents. Here are a few options:

- When you go to your child in the middle of the night, keep the lights off. Don't make this a time to talk or play, and gradually shorten the feeding time. Over time, many children come to understand that you will go in and reassure them, and that their job is to settle to sleep. Eventually, they will wake up and fall back asleep without you. If they don't fully wake up, they are more likely to resettle themselves. This is a gradual and gentle (and therefore much slower) method of breaking the habit of nighttime wakings.
- Some parents will let their child cry for a set period of time, perhaps five or 10 minutes, before going to her. Do not pick up your child or play with her, but instead calmly tuck her back into bed. Once you have reassured your child that you are nearby, again go out of the room for another few minutes. Continue this until she falls asleep on her own. You can gradually increase the amount of time you wait until going to your child. (If at any time you have concerns for your child's safety or well-being, go and check on her immediately.) You may find that it takes nerves of steel to listen to crying, but this method is reported to be a quicker solution to nighttime wakings.
- If your child is big enough and out of the crib, you can make a bed for her on the floor of your bedroom. If she wakes, she can come and sleep in your room.
- After making sure their child is not ill or injured, some parents will call out to reassure her but will not go into her room.
- Some parents will get up and immediately reassure their child every time she wakes up. They tell her it's time for sleep, and then go back to their own room.
- Some parents sleep with their child every night. This is called co-sleeping. How well this is working for parent and child will need a periodic review.

▶ **Q: "My child is up at five o'clock every morning and then napping at eight. At that point I'm tired, but I'm up for the day. What should I be doing?"**

▶ **A:** Your child may simply be waking up at five and now sees that as a drawn-out play period before falling asleep again at eight to finish her nighttime sleep. Try delaying going to your child for a few minutes when she wakes at five to see if she will fall asleep again. If this doesn't work, try delaying her morning naptime by 10 minutes a day until she's having her nap in the late morning or even afternoon. This may help her to sleep longer at night.

For further information, one reference that some parents report is useful is: *Solve Your Child's Sleep Problems* by Richard Ferber, MD.

Getting Ready to Use the Toilet

Most children master this skill between the ages of two and three. Staying dry at night often takes longer, sometimes up to six years of age. You may hear that toilet learning is easy for some children and that it happens quickly. But for most toddlers it takes between two weeks and six months to learn, so patience is very important.

Being able to use the toilet is a stage of development that each child will reach at a different time. Try not to be pressured into training your child before he's ready, since this will only make the process longer, more difficult, and frustrating for both of you. Toilet training can be a very positive experience for your child, since he will discover a new skill and take pride in his ability.

Key Strategies for Toilet Training Your Child
- Start only when your child shows you that he's ready.
- Let your child be in charge of his toileting, but do your part by having a potty close by, having a general routine with potty reminders, and encouraging him with his successes.
- Do not pressure your child in any way. Keep the toilet a battle-free zone and yourself neutral.

So how do you know when your toddler is both able and ready to use the potty? Ask yourself the following questions:

☑ Does my child stay dry for a few hours at a time or wake up dry from a nap occasionally? This shows that he has the physical ability to control his bladder.

☑ Does my child indicate in some way that he's aware of when he urinates or has a bowel movement (BM)? Some signs could be that he goes into a corner or squats to have a BM, or comments on soiled diapers, or has an "accident" without diapers on and is bothered by, or comments on, the urine.

☑ Can my child follow simple directions and communicate basic needs, such as "I want milk," "I'm cold," or "Come to the bathroom"?

☑ Is my toddler able to pull down his pants and underwear by himself?

I Think My Child Is Ready

If you answered "yes" to most of the questions above, here are some ideas for getting started on toilet training:

• Wait for a stable time in your child's life for the best results. Toilet learning is best started when there are no other stresses going on. Stresses are things like going to a new daycare, a new sibling in the house, moving homes, illness in the family, or other family changes.

• If you are comfortable doing so, let your toddler watch you sit on the toilet and explain what you're doing. Observing a same-sex parent or sibling urinate is worth a thousand words of explaining how to do it.

• Reading books together about toilet learning can help a toddler get ready to understand this skill. Another way is to have your child put his dolls on the potty and teach them how to use it.

• Talk about using the toilet and how he will be "grown up like Mommy and Daddy" or an older sibling. Help him to see that it's a good change. He won't have to wear diapers anymore, or he'll be able to wear underwear with cartoons on them like big kids.

• If possible, let your child pick out his own potty (available in most stores that carry children's supplies or children's consignment shops) and place it next to the toilet. If your child is interested in the big toilet, you can buy a toilet seat that fits on top of your regular seat. This seat should be stable so that it doesn't easily move when your toddler is on it. You will also need to have a stable stool for your child to use to get up onto the toilet.

• Once you have the potty, encourage your child to sit on it, play with it, or move it around. Let him claim the potty as "his." Something that he feels he controls and owns will be more user-friendly than an object that is tightly controlled by a parent.

• Resist the urge to use sweet treats as rewards for using the potty. Your child will begin to view sweet food as a reward, and as he uses the toilet regularly, you will be filling him up with candy. As one mother says, *"As soon as Suzie figured out the Smartie® system she would squeeze out two drops just to get a treat."* If you do use a reward system, try stars on a chart for every successful toilet trip, a coin in the piggy bank, or a made-up song of success.

• When starting toilet training, offer your child training pants, also known as "pull ups." These pants can be easily and quickly pulled down and back up again. Dress your child in easy-to-remove clothes with elastic waists that can be

pulled down in a hurry. It may also help to let your toddler go without pants around the easily cleaned parts of the house or in the yard. That way, as soon as he gets the urge, he can sit on the potty right away.

- There are many different approaches to toilet training. One is to watch the clock and put your child (if willing) onto the toilet at regular times, every hour or two. Another is to watch your child for signs of needing to go and then take him to the potty. Whichever method you choose, don't force him to the toilet. Instead, suggest and encourage. For example, say, *"I'm going to the bathroom, do you want to come too?"* or *"Your potty is waiting for you"* or *"It's potty time."* Remember to place your child on the toilet immediately upon waking, as he will often urinate then.

- When your child is successful, try to focus your praise on the act rather than on him being "good." Encouraging comments such as *"How wonderful that you went pee on the potty"* instead of *"Good boy"* help him to see that using the toilet is the goal. It also shows that success (or lack of it) doesn't make him a good or bad person in his parent's eyes. Never scold, belittle, or shame your child for accidents, since this may make him even more hesitant to try again.

- If your child gets bored on the toilet, perhaps when waiting for a bowel movement, give him something to do. Let him read a book or play with a small toy.
- Communicate with other caregivers about how to handle your child's toilet training, since consistency is important for success.
- When your toddler is using the potty at least some of the time, take him shopping for new underwear. Toddlers are often very fond of their clothes, and wearing new underwear like big kids can be encouraging.

This Seems to Take Forever!

- **Stay relaxed!** Praise your child for his efforts and try not to be disappointed over accidents. Try not to show any emotional reaction to soiled pants— just clean it up and encourage your child to use the potty next time. **Think of toilet training as learning how to run. You wouldn't scold for a fall, so don't for a soiled diaper either.**
- Expect accidents. Even older children have them, especially when they're sick, cold, or very involved in play.
- Be prepared to do extra laundry and roll up the expensive area rugs for a while.
- Be prepared to continue toilet training away from home. Before you go out with your child, find the locations of bathrooms. If you're spending the night away from home, bring the potty.
- If your child is dealing with a major change or stress in his life, be prepared to go back to diapers for a while. Talk about the stress with your child and let him know that he can go back to using the toilet when he's ready.
- Sometimes children want to go back to wearing diapers for no apparent reason. If this happens, remember that your toddler is learning a new skill. It's normal to go one step forward and two steps back.
- **Be patient!** Remember that each child is unique and will learn and develop at his own pace. Being able to use the toilet at an early age has no bearing on how smart or capable he is. Just as an early walker is not necessarily an early reader, neither is a late toilet trainer behind on other skills.

Sexual Development

The way that you touch and talk about your child's body sends her important messages, even at a very early age. When you change diapers in a matter-of-fact way, you are telling your child that the area between her legs is simply another part of her body. Toilet training, if dealt with in a calm and patient manner, communicates that elimination is normal and healthy. Showing disgust with diapers or shame and discomfort with cleaning the genitals teaches your child that this area is somehow bad or "dirty." Remember that at this age children understand more than just words. They need to first *feel* comfortable more than they need to understand detailed sexual development.

As you talk to your child, name the parts of the body. Along with elbows, knees, and nose, don't forget the penis or vulva. Your child learns that she can talk about these parts of the body as comfortably as the ear or foot. It also makes it easier to discuss sexual development and how to say no to improper touching.

Tips on Communicating a Healthy, Relaxed Attitude

- Deal with your child's genitals, elimination, and exploration as normal and healthy.
- Use accurate terms for her body parts to help your child learn this language.
- Answer her questions clearly and simply.

▶ **Q: "Is it all right for us to be naked in front of our two-year-old?"**

▶ **A:** The answer to this question lies with you and your child. Some adults and some children are much shyer than others are, and everyone has a right to privacy. Is your child bothered by or aware of your nudity? If so, then you should be putting on some clothes. At about age three children will begin to be curious about your genitals and may ask questions when they see them, or even try to touch them. The question of when to stop open nudity in the family is one of individual levels of privacy, not of age or gender. **As your child becomes sensitive about her privacy, it is your job, as the adult, to support and accept this.** Whoever says no to the nudity is to be respected, and you may even find that it's you who wants privacy.

Communicate in a calm and positive way when you talk about nudity and personal privacy. *"Mommy likes to have privacy when she has a bath, thank you,"* or *"I'm changing right now—I'll be out when I'm dressed."* Older toddlers are beginning to understand privacy. If your child sees you naked, react calmly by explaining that grown-up people like to have privacy occasionally, just like she will at times.

▶ **Q: "Now that our child is out of his crib, he's come into our bedroom while we're having sex. What should we do?"**

▶ **A:** The first thing to remember is that neither of you has done anything wrong. Calmly guide your child out of the room and explain that you would like privacy right now. If he seems upset, explain that you weren't hurting each other (which it may have looked or sounded like to him). If you react in a calm, non-embarrassed manner, your child is likely to forget all about seeing you. Installing a lock on your bedroom door may be a good idea at this time.

Masturbation

Although children as young as seven months will explore their genitals, it is more common in two- to three-year-olds. This kind of investigation begins as a natural curiosity about their body. Just as your toddler put her finger into her navel and played with her toes, so will she touch her genitals. This is natural and normal, and should not be discouraged. Once discovered, it doesn't take long for the toddler to realize that this touching feels good. Your reaction to your toddler's masturbation or touching of her genitals is important to her developing attitude toward sexuality. The best approach you can take is to ignore the activity; she is not doing anything wrong. By punishing or shaming your child, you are making the forbidden activity even more enticing and causing her to feel confusion or guilt about her genitals. If your child is touching herself in public, and is old enough to understand you, simply explain what you

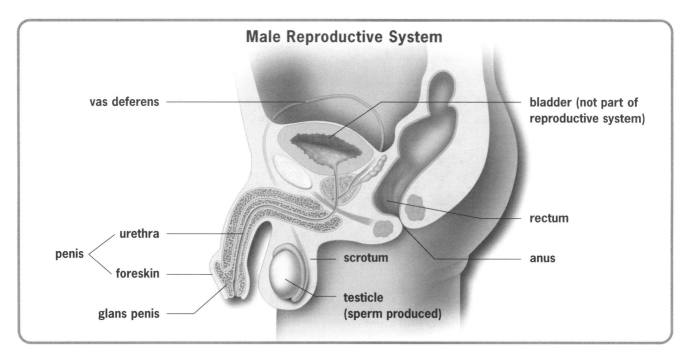

Male Reproductive System

vas deferens

bladder (not part of reproductive system)

rectum

penis
- urethra
- foreskin

scrotum

anus

glans penis

testicle (sperm produced)

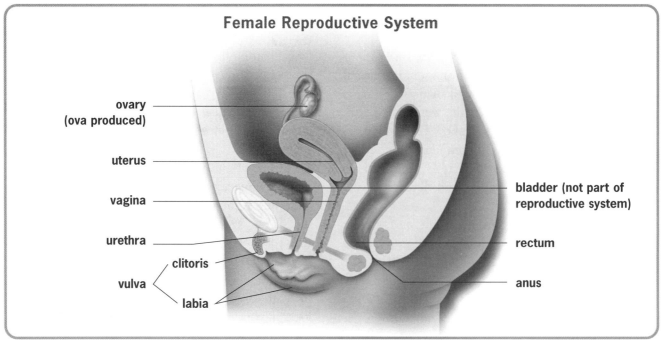

Female Reproductive System

ovary (ova produced)

uterus

vagina

bladder (not part of reproductive system)

urethra

rectum

clitoris

vulva

anus

labia

can do in public and what you do at home. *"Some things are private. You can do that at home in your room—how about playing with this toy for now?"*

If you find your child (usually three and older) exploring his genitals, also known as "playing doctor," with another child of similar age, try not to be shocked or react negatively. Simply comment on what they are doing: *"I see you two are looking at each other's penises."* Let them know that their genitals are private parts of their bodies and should not be touched by other people. Then distract the children and go on to other activities. Do not attach shame, guilt, or negative feelings to their interest in their bodies. This is a good opportunity to encourage your child to come and tell you if he is uncomfortable with another child's curiosity or exploring. *"You can come and tell me and I won't be mad. I'll help you and your friend find another game or something else to do."*

Some children who have been abused will become abusive to other children who are the same age or younger. An older child should not be exploring genitals with a younger child, as the toddler usually sees him as more powerful. Talk to your doctor or public health nurse if you have concerns about your child being touched inappropriately by another child. Do not leave the children alone together. Calmly talk with your child about what happened in order to get the facts, and explain that no one should touch or look at his genitals without his permission.

Children Learn Through Play

One of the ways your child learns and develops is by playing. As she collects objects to put in a container, she may find that some fit and others don't. She may be able to squeeze some things and force them in, but she'll also learn that this doesn't work with other objects.

This is a good example of how a child learns about space, textures, shapes, sizes, and directions. When she plays, she's doing what comes naturally. At the same time, she's building a good foundation for learning in the future.

Ideas like colour and shape are learned through normal conversation. *"Do you want the red cup or the blue one? I think the square container will make a good*

sand castle." Mathematical ideas are also learned naturally, as your toddler counts the apple slices you give her, plays with blocks, or digs in the sand.

You can help your child learn by encouraging and supporting her natural desire to understand how the world works. She doesn't need to be told— she discovers on her own through play. You can help by making sure her environment is safe to explore, and then stepping back and watching her learn for herself.

Playing has a vital role in your child's growth and development. It may be more accurate to say that your child is busy learning rather than busy playing. **Play is a child's way of discovering and understanding not only what is in the world, but also how everything and everybody relates to each other.**

Concepts such as space, in, out, big, small, far or near, real or pretend seem simple to us. To your toddler these ideas are completely unknown and must be learned by experimenting with objects and people in her environment.

Your child drops her spoon from her high chair and plays babbling games with you. Your toddler pretends to talk on the phone and takes her doll for a ride in the wagon. The two-year-olds in the play group sit around in the sandbox, observing one another as they shovel sand into buckets. These are all important activities in a toddler's life, and help her to understand complex concepts.

What Children Learn When They Play

- **How things work.** Toddlers learn that things can still exist even when they can't see them. Peek-a-boo or hide-and-seek are just two examples. Toddlers also learn that objects and people are unique and separate from themselves.
- **The nature of materials and how they relate to each other.** Some examples are glue, wool, paper, water, and paint. Your child learns that some materials can stick together and some can't; some things make colourful artwork when mixed with water and others don't.
- **Concepts.** Anything they can shape, pour, or measure helps children learn concepts such as more/less, larger/smaller, empty/full. They also give children a sense of control. Examples include sand, water, clay, and playdough.
- **Rhythm.** Musical instruments let children experiment with rhythm and sound and help them to improve their memory and anticipation. Sing songs or dance to music together, and let them bang spoons on the table or drum to make music.
- **Words and ideas.** Books help children use and understand language. They learn to look at pictures, and to understand that pictures stand for something that is real. Children develop ideas and acquire language through all kinds of play, and through communicating and interacting.
- **How to cooperate and socialize with others.** Any time children play together they practise waiting turns, sharing, and interacting. It takes time, but toddlers eventually learn these social skills.
- **How to solve problems.** Construction toys help children develop their coordination, learn numbers and science concepts, and solve problems as they build higher and more complicated structures. Examples include blocks and building sets.
- **How to use their imaginations.** Pretend play materials encourage children to use their imagination and help them understand the world by trying out roles. Examples include dress-up clothes, dolls, kitchen sets, cash registers, dramatic figures, and telephones.
- **To be creative.** Art materials help creativity and build skills that lead to writing and reading. Examples include paper, paint, brushes, crayons, and markers. (Store materials, especially scissors, carefully.)

- **How to use their bodies.** Active play builds strong muscles and balance and gives children confidence. Examples of active toys include climbing frames, slides, swings, balls, wagons, and riding toys. Playing with smaller objects helps with the development of fine motor skills and hand-eye coordination.
- **That they are capable and can make things happen.** Playing increases children's confidence and self-esteem.

Ways to Encourage Your Child to Play

Childproof an area for your child to play in. Let him explore and play without restrictions. For ideas about childproofing your house, see the section on safety on page 95.

- Let play be free or directed by your child. Children learn best when they can choose what they want to do. You can be involved by following the cues your child gives you, such as *"Roll ball, Mommy,"* or you can guide your child by suggesting activities that are a natural extension of what he's doing. If your child is shaping playdough, you may want to say, *"That looks like a car—would you like to make a hill for that car to drive over?"*
- Let play be unstructured. Toddlers are not able to understand the rules of a game or to act out anything but the simplest story.
- Provide a variety of toys and playthings appropriate for your child's age.
- Put toys out on a rotating basis. Children enjoy new things and may become overwhelmed if they have too many toys to choose from all at once.

- Play with your toddler. You may not always have the time to be down on your hands and knees with him, but you can play singing games and guessing games while you're doing other things.
- Be ready to stop playing or to put away some toys if your child looks away or cries. He may be telling you that he's tired, hungry, or overstimulated.
- Take him outside and watch him crawl over logs, inspect insects, pick grass or stones, and generally explore nature.
- Let your toddler help wash dishes, tear lettuce, dig in the garden, make beds, or whatever else interests him. What looks like work to you may be fun for him.
- Encourage your child to do artwork, using his own ideas. This may be gluing clippings of colourful paper onto a board or smearing paint with his hands. He may need your assistance to get started and to understand what the materials can do as he pastes, colours, or cuts. Then, let him be creative with your encouragement. (Remember, even child scissors can hurt.)
- Show your child that you value his play by giving him lots of praise and encouragement. Tell others how good he is at climbing, painting, or building with blocks and proudly show his work.
- Be playful. If you like to sing or dance or do puzzles, do these things with your child.

Types of Play

Children can learn through different kinds of play. You'll probably see your toddler do all of the following:
- **Solitary play** is when your toddler plays by herself. All children like to do this at times.
- **Social bids** are the first steps toward having fun with others. Well before the age of two, most children will offer each other toys, looks, or words. It's their way of communicating.
- Before the age of two, children engage in **imitative play**. In other words, they copy each other. One toddler starts to jump and soon they're all doing it. Or you are folding clothes and your child tries to do the same.
- Babies and toddlers also enjoy **parallel play**. This is when they play side by side without interacting. They will, however, observe each other and often imitate actions.

- As children get older, they start to explore **cooperative play**. Some children will help to build a block village or take their stuffed animals to the doctor. Many children are not ready for this kind of play until they're three or older.

Watching Television

Television can be a very useful tool for education and entertainment. We are able to see places and things and experience situations that may not be available in our communities. But too much TV or unsupervised watching can be a negative influence in a child's life rather than a positive one. If your child is watching TV, ask yourself whether he spends enough time playing, interacting, speaking, imagining, creating, or being physically active. (Excessive television viewing has also been linked to obesity later in life.) Also consider that TV may take you away from spending time playing with your child.

According to research, the majority of children in Canada will spend more time watching television than they will spend at school. Research indicates that when children watch a lot of television they are more verbally and physically aggressive. They also are less creative, have more rigid ideas about sex roles, and are not as strong at problem solving.

Researchers suspect that young children do not learn much from watching television. While children watch television, they use only two senses: sight and hearing. Toddlers learn most when they are using all their senses when playing or interacting with others.

Even TV shows that are created for young children often move too quickly and have plots that are too complex for a toddler. Consequently they are simply bombarded with colours, movement, and sound. Think about what you would like your child to gain from TV time. If your child turns on the TV when he's bored, try to offer alternatives. He may prefer to colour pictures, read a story, or play outside.

Some books recommend that parents sit with their children and discuss what they are watching, how they feel about the program, and if it makes sense to them in the real world. This may be effective with older children, but toddlers are too young to focus on a program, process the messages, and then discuss it with you. Delay watching television as long as possible with this age group, and once you do allow television, then be very selective about what your child watches and how much she watches.

Some Ideas About Watching Television

- Your toddler is watching you while you are watching television. Set a good example by spending your free time with your family reading, exercising, talking, being involved in a hobby, playing sports, or listening to music.
- Choose shows that are focused on education for young children. Be careful if you leave the room—the program you have chosen may end and be followed by an adult program.

- Remember that you are in charge of what shows your child watches, since she is not old enough to choose programs that are best for her. If you have a VCR, record children's programs or movies so that you can have them on hand.
- Keep the television off during family mealtimes and make conversation a priority. Arrange furniture so that it is not around the television.
- Find ways other than television viewing to reward your child ("*If you eat all of your beans you can watch* Cinderella"). Using television as a prize can make it seem even more important to children.
- Watch television with your child, not only to keep him company but also to see what it is he is absorbing, disturbed by, or enjoying. If you watch a show about dinosaurs, help the learning by going to the library for books about dinosaurs.

▶ **Q: "I like to watch the news when I get home, but I also want to visit with my two-year-old. How do I do both?"**

▶ **A:** You have a few options. One is to watch the later news when your toddler is in bed. Another is to tape the news if you have a VCR, and again, watch it when your child is in bed or busy with some other activity. If you watch only the business or political news, it may not be a problem having your child watch with you, but general daily news with disturbing and at times violent scenes may be too graphic for a young child. Some children will experience nightmares if they view upsetting scenes.

▶ **Q: "Our one-year-old regularly sits with his big sister and wants to watch her shows, which I think are too adult for him. I'm not sure what to do, because I don't want to make his sister resent him being around."**

▶ **A:** This is a fairly common problem in households with children of varying ages. It's a good idea to get your older child involved in the plan to protect the younger children in the house. Again, if you have a VCR you can record the program and your daughter can watch it when your toddler isn't around. You can also work out a plan where the nightly bath occurs at the same time as your daughter's favourite show, so your toddler is out of the room. Or if your daughter is willing, she can give up watching the show in favour of a more enjoyable activity with the rest of the family.

Your Child's Development from Six Months to One Year

Your child's first year is an exciting time for your whole family. She moves from being a tiny newborn to a competent person who can sit, and may be crawling or walking. She grows fast—about an inch a month—and, by the time she's a year old, she's probably tripled her birth weight.

You and your child will spend this year building your relationship. She's learning to "read" your words, gestures, and facial expressions, and she knows how to get your attention—sometimes by smiling, babbling, and kicking her legs; sometimes by crying; and sometimes by screaming or shouting. You get her attention by talking and singing to her, and by cuddling and playing games with her.

At this age, your child is also learning to talk. She imitates the sounds you make, has "conversations" with you, and is learning language by listening to, and interacting with, family members. She may not speak, but she understands more and more of what you say.

If you speak more than one language in your home, your child will probably learn them both (or all) by the time she's a toddler. Don't worry about confusing her. Toddlers who learn more than one language from birth are often very skilled at switching back and forth to communicate with different people in different situations.

Speaking of differences, around this time you may be noticing how different your child is from other children her age. She may be sleeping and napping on a regular schedule—or not. She may be faster or slower than others at learning to crawl or walk. She may be comforted easily or cry for long periods. And she may sleep for a long time, or stay awake for hours. If you want to get a little more sleep, see page 8 for more information.

Don't worry about comparing your toddler with others. Your child is unique, and the most important thing is to respond to her unique signals. This lets her know that you understand her and that she's important to you. It teaches her that she can trust the people in her world—and trust is the basis for all the other learning she will do.

During the end of her first year, you may notice that your child seems upset when you leave her in someone else's care, even if that person is someone she knows. This can make separation difficult. However, it shows that your child is attached to you and knows the difference between different people.

Your child can now show you a thinking, feeling person. By playing with her, talking to her, encouraging and praising her, explaining how and why things work, and giving her lots of love and attention, you can make sure she has a happy, healthy start in life.

Physical Development

Your Child at Six Months

At four to six months, your child's birth weight is generally doubled. The average height for a girl is 55 cm (21.5 in) and for a boy, it's 57 cm (22.5 in). Front teeth may be showing. (This could happen as late as 12 months). Take your child for her six-month immunizations. This should be her third set.

Provide plenty of safe space where your child can practise movement and show him that you are delighted with all his new skills. Breastfeeding is generally going well. If he's drinking from a bottle, he may be able to hold the bottle but would prefer to have it held. Propping a bottle can be dangerous to your child and is not recommended.

Remember: Everything will go into your child's mouth. Choking and poisoning can happen. Child-proof your house so he can explore as much as possible. Also, car safety continues to be very important—car accidents are a leading cause of injury at this age. See page 115 for information on infant seats.

What Your Child May Be Learning at Six Months	What You Can Do to Help— Be sure to celebrate new skills
PHYSICAL DEVELOPMENT	
Sits fairly well without support.	Play "riding the horse" games with your child sitting on your knee or foot as you *gently* bounce him up and down while supporting him under the arms. These games will help him develop balance.
If held in a standing position, can support almost all of her own weight on her legs.	Help her to strengthen her legs by supporting her as she tries to "walk" or as she pushes with her feet on your lap.
Rolls from back to tummy and can lift his chest and upper tummy off the ground with his arms when lying on his stomach.	Place him on his tummy for some play time, making sure that you are close by.
Begins to move things from one hand to the other and will bang objects together.	Pass her toys, one first then another, so that she will move the first toy to her spare hand.
May have two lower teeth in, and begins to bite and chew. Can just hold a cracker in her fingers to feed herself.	If new teeth are bothering your child, give her firm objects designed for teething to chew on.
Likes objects that fit inside each other, such as pots and pans.	Give him objects to grasp, manipulate, mouth, stack, shake, and bang. These include nesting cups, rattles, and plastic bowls of different sizes.
Drops objects, knocks blocks down.	Provide an environment that has many interesting things to see, touch, and taste.
Is beginning to reach out for objects with more determination, but still can't usually grasp anything that is moving.	Provide lots of toys, like balls, sturdy toys on wheels, blocks, nesting toys, and simple puzzles, as well as household items. Encourage your child to stretch and reach for toys by placing them just out of her reach at times.
Picks up objects with thumb and first finger. Hands are getting stronger.	Give him washcloths, sponges, containers, and bath toys that float and provide him with an opportunity to pour, squirt, or drip water while in the bath.
Explores objects by putting them in her mouth.	**Make sure that all poisons and cleaning fluids are locked up and well out of reach.**

SOCIAL AND EMOTIONAL DEVELOPMENT

May begin to fear strangers, since she is now recognizing them as different from family members. She may even be reluctant to go to family members (such as Grandma) if she hasn't seen them for a while.	Support your child if she is afraid of strangers—don't force her to be held or approached if she's frightened. Be aware that this is a difficult time for her to be left with people whom she may view as strangers, such as a new babysitter or someone she hasn't seen for a while.
She's forming specific attachments to her caregivers and may not want to be separated from them.	When you pick her up from child care, spend a short time visiting before you leave so she can get used to the change.
Will start holding out her arms to be picked up.	Be surprised and delighted with her new skill.
May begin imitating others, such as sticking out her tongue or opening her mouth.	Play face-to-face games—scrunch up your nose, stick out your tongue—and see if she copies you.
May easily swing between emotions such as laughing and crying with little reason.	Be understanding.
Is developing a sense of humour, and may laugh when her head is hidden under a blanket or when she sees a funny face.	Help your child to look at herself in the mirror.
Knows what she likes and dislikes.	Offer choices that you are comfortable with.

LANGUAGE DEVELOPMENT

Begins to imitate sounds he hears.	Respond to the sounds he makes. Make a game of imitating your child's sounds and facial expressions.
Will be laughing, yelling, blowing raspberries, and cooing.	Laugh when she makes a funny sound—let her know that you think communicating is fun.
Babbles and makes sounds like *da*, *ma*, *ga*, *ka*, *hi*.	Talk to him in simple sentences about what each of you is doing. Ask, *"What's that?"* as you point to his teddy. Wait for a moment and say, *"It's Teddy!"* Your child will start pointing at things and using his voice to ask a question even though he might not use words. Children love books. Hold your child on your lap and read to him. Use catalogues, magazines, picture books, and photograph albums. Talk about the pictures.
Enjoys hearing his own sounds, and may "talk" to toys or a mirror.	Sing songs and recite nursery rhymes to your child. He will learn to recognize and repeat them.
Looks at you when you say his name.	Name the people and foods that are around. Repeat names of body parts, such as nose, eyes, mouth.

What Your Child May Be Learning at Six Months	What You Can Do to Help— Be sure to celebrate new skills
INTELLECTUAL DEVELOPMENT	
May briefly look for something he has dropped, but will very soon forget about it.	Expect attachment to special toys or blankets to develop soon.
May recognize something that is partially hidden.	Play games where objects are lost from sight and then reappear, such as a car going behind a box or a train disappearing behind the couch and coming out the other side. Play hiding games. Hide a toy under a towel while your child watches. Let a small part peek out. Ask your child where the toy is and show pleasure when he finds it.
May move quickly from one activity to another.	Encourage him to learn concepts like *in* and *out* by giving him containers with things to put in and dump out, like clothespins, blocks, and balls.
Is beginning to do two activities at the same time, such as banging a spoon and shouting.	Play music. Your child may like to bang a spoon on a container to the beat of the music.
Becomes conscious of having only one mother and father.	Hold her and cuddle her as she begins to understand her world and feel safe in it. Welcome that special smile she has just for you.
Understanding of words increases.	Use the word "*No*" only when necessary (e.g., there's danger) so that a range of ideas are encouraged.
Enjoys fun activities.	Play games like peek-a-boo. Cover your face with your hands, then remove your hands and say "*Peek-a-boo, I see you!*"
Notices how things are different.	Give him various foods, toys, and fabrics with assorted textures so that he can feel the differences.

Your Child at One Year

At one year, your child's birth weight is generally tripled. The average child is about 75 to 82 centimetres (29 to 32 inches) tall and she may have six to eight teeth. Take your child for her one-year immunizations. This should be her fourth set of immunizations.

By now he will have the same ideas of good and bad smells as you do. He will usually prefer salty, sweet, and fatty tastes. He will push unwanted objects away. He will understand that some objects make more noise than others do—he'll choose a spoon instead of a soft teddy bear.

Very soon, your child will pull up on anything that's handy. Childproof now!

What Your Child May Be Learning at One Year	What You Can Do to Help
PHYSICAL DEVELOPMENT	
As her hands become more skilled, she will be using her mouth less to explore objects. Safety is still important.	She will begin to play with toys more appropriately, by pushing a train, hugging a doll, or pushing buttons on pop-up toys.
May creep on his belly at about nine months, then crawl, either on hands and knees, hands and feet, or by scooting along on his bottom.	Help him to stand alone by gradually decreasing the amount of support you provide. **Gate stairs, top and bottom, since your toddler may suddenly decide to start climbing.**
Takes first steps, cruises around holding onto furniture, may be walking holding a hand. About half will be able to walk at 13 months, but most will fall often.	Arrange furniture so that she can cruise while holding onto something sturdy. Gradually move things farther apart so that she has to take more steps to reach the next support. **Now she'll be getting into your drinks or snacks on the coffee table and anything she can get to. Move around at your child's eye level to see what she sees. Childproof now!**
Usually can eat well with his fingers and drink from a cup.	Allow your child to feed himself, even if he makes a mess. Feed your child where cleanup is simple. **Be sure to give him only foods that do not pose a choking hazard. Do not give him popcorn, nuts, or other small pieces of food that he could choke on.**
Pulls up to stand, but might need help coming down. **Make sure that any furniture that could tip over is securely fastened to the wall. Lamp cords should be taped to table legs or moved so that your child can't pull lamps off of tables. Tablecloths are not safe, since your child can pull hot items down on himself.**	Help your child to walk by: holding her hands and walking together; providing toys she can push along with her; having her wear socks with non-slip bottoms or soft shoes so that she has fewer falls.
May try to build a two-block tower, but will usually fail.	Encourage her to try again.
Can put cubes into a cup.	Give him toys or household items that can be put into larger containers and taken out again, such as small blocks into a bucket or dry cereal into a cup.
When turning pages in a book, will usually turn many at a time.	Read with your child. Let him choose books and turn the pages.

What Your Child May Be Learning at One Year	What You Can Do to Help

SOCIAL AND EMOTIONAL DEVELOPMENT

May begin to explore and separate from you for brief periods, but will use you as the safe base if away from home. May cling to you in new situations as his fear of strangers and strange places is increased.	If moving to a new child care provider, spend a short time with your child and reassure her that you will return.
Loves being the centre of attention.	Let him help with feeding and dressing as much as he is able to. Give praise frequently. *"You picked up bunny all by yourself! Wonderful!"*
Will enjoy familiar places, such as home or Grandma's house, more than new places.	If you are travelling with your child, bring lots of familiar toys and home objects.
May have a security blanket or a favourite toy that she keeps close at all times.	Let her have a security blanket or toy if she wants—this will help her to be more confident and independent.
Shows emotions such as jealousy, anger, fear, or affection.	Describe her feelings while she is experiencing them. *"You're sad right now because your dad had to leave."*
May give you a hug or kiss if you ask.	Give rag dolls, baby dolls, and stuffed animals and play at activities such as rocking the bear, feeding the doll, tucking the animals into bed. These games help your child to express his emotions as actions.
Enjoys being with other children, but won't play with them; may hit, grab, or push.	Change to another activity if she begins pushing or grabbing.

LANGUAGE DEVELOPMENT

May say three to five words besides *"mama"* and *"dada."* Copies simple sounds like *"bye-bye"* and may wave. May imitate animal sounds like *"moo"* or *"meow."*	Continue to read with your child. Let him choose books and turn the pages.
Will understand the meaning of many words, even if she is unable to say them. Understanding always comes before talking.	Talk with your child as much as possible and gradually increase the number of things you are naming each day. Wait for her to tell you what she wants before you respond automatically.

LANGUAGE DEVELOPMENT

Is beginning to understand basic sentences. If you ask a question like *"Where is your bottle?"* he will look or point in the direction of his bottle.	When your child babbles or talks to you, help him by showing that you hear him, and then say the correct word, for example, *"BaBa" "Yes, that's a bottle"* or *"Dada" "Yes, that's Daddy."*
Stops what she is doing, maybe very briefly, when you say *"No."* Shakes her head *no*.	Use *"No"* in relation to safety and when really needed.

INTELLECTUAL DEVELOPMENT

Knows that people and objects still exist when they are out of sight.	Play games where she has to find objects that are hidden: *"Where's the teddy? Let's go look."*
Points to parts of her body when asked.	Read books together and have your child point out pictures. Reading together helps your child to develop her memory and attention span.
Recognizes her name and may come if you use it.	Use her name when talking. Know that she will not come all the time.
Knows about cause and effect, for example, knows that things fall when she drops them.	Talk with your child about what happened: *"You dropped your teddy, so now Teddy's on the floor."*
Imitates your actions. If you clap, she claps.	Clap hands, sing songs, and play patty cake together.
Will look for a lost toy with more determination. Has an excellent visual memory and may be able to find things that you have forgotten about.	Ask for her help if you are looking for something: *"Where is kitty?"* or *"Help me to find your shoes."* **Store dangerous items so your child does not know where they are.**
May be able to put two ideas together, such as going into the hall to get the train and bringing it back into the playroom.	Help your child string thoughts together by suggesting activities with two actions, such as *"Let's throw the ball and chase it"* or *"Let's find Teddy and feed him"* or *"Let's dump out the toys and put them back in again."*
May be able to leave an activity and return to it to continue playing.	

Your Child's Development from One Year to Two Years

The second year of life means huge changes for children and, often, challenges for parents. This is the time when your child becomes very active and more independent. He will start running, jumping, speaking in full sentences, and ask for things in new ways.

During the second year his physical growth slows down. He may gain only 1.5 to 2.5 kgs (3 to 5 lbs) this year. The way he looks will change. His muscles will develop, and so will his taste for certain kinds of food. Toddlers generally eat what the family eats, but they do have definite preferences and want to make their own choices.

Your one-year-old still learns by exploring through all his senses. He's interested in active play and wants to practise new skills. This gives him a sense of competence and confidence, and helps him feel more independent. You may notice him starting to want to do things his way, including saying "No" or refusing your requests. Easy choices and encouragement will help him to move forward.

By the middle of their second year, many toddlers have powerful feelings and start to express them strongly. Their relationship with you also changes as they learn to do certain things themselves. Sometimes they may seem to resent your help. At other times they want you to assist them. For example, your child may insist on putting on his own shoes and then want you to button his jacket. This is a good example of how toddlers often move quickly from feeling independent to needing reassurance and comfort.

Remember that toddlers are only starting to understand their own feelings. They haven't yet learned to appreciate other people's feelings. If this leads to conflicts (for example, your child takes a toy from another child), help him understand that his actions affect other people. Talk to him about his feelings, name them, and accept them. Explain how someone else might feel, and be patient. Your toddler will need a great deal of experience before he learns how his actions affect other people. Children need to learn and practise not taking toys or not hitting; they are not born knowing these things.

Some of this learning comes from playing make believe, which many children start to do at about 18 months. They may comfort a teddy bear, encourage dolls to hold hands, or feed someone an imaginary supper. This helps them understand what it's like to be someone else and, eventually, to learn about how other people feel.

Whatever he does or doesn't do, it's very important, at this age, that your toddler gets the love and attention to feel secure about his relationship with you. He also needs gentle guidance to help him develop and practise new skills. You can help by giving him his own responsibilities and including him in things like grocery shopping and dish washing. Whatever you do, let him know that spending time together is something you enjoy.

Your Child at 18 Months

Young children between one and two years of age are learning independence and are very exploratory in their approach to the world. They are usually fully mobile, but fall often. Always think about safety.

First molars may be coming in between 12 and 18 months and cuspid teeth will arrive between 16 and 23 months. It will be time for his fifth set of immunizations.

What Your Child May Be Learning at Eighteen Months	What You Can Do to Help
PHYSICAL DEVELOPMENT	
Can walk forward, backward, and sideways. His legs may be less widely spaced as his centre of gravity changes and he finds it easier to balance on his feet.	Go for short walks; bring a stroller for when he gets tired. **Cover any sharp edges on furniture.** **Cover fireplaces.**
May be running, but will fall often. Can pull a toy on a string, push a walk-along toy, or ride a sit-and-push-with-your-feet car.	Sit-and-ride toys help her to develop balance and learn how to move around things that are in her way.
Can stand on one foot with support.	Simple hopping games are a fun way to build this skill. If he becomes frustrated, change the activity.
Will find it hard to walk and carry something at the same time.	Hold her hand to keep her steady or help her find another way to carry things.
If going up and down stairs, will usually do it on his hands and knees and tummy.	Hold his hand so he can walk up or down stairs; he will place both feet on each step before advancing. Gate stairs so they will be safe when you are not there.
Is able to get going better than she can stop. May rush to a new place and then sink to the ground once she's there.	Give your child a small cloth or paper (not plastic) bag to collect pebbles, leaves, grass, or anything else you can think of. This simple activity helps her practise stopping, starting, bending over, and standing again without falling.
Can usually stack two blocks.	Use empty milk containers to make a fun set of blocks.
Can usually throw a ball, though not well.	Roll and throw a ball by sitting across from each other on the floor and rolling, kicking, or throwing a light ball back and forth.
SOCIAL AND EMOTIONAL DEVELOPMENT	
Is able to experiment with objects and people to see how they work for him. This may feel like manipulation to you, but it's experimentation to him.	Work this into your dressing routine: *"You get this, I will get that…"*
Enjoys the company of other children, but usually does not play with them unless it's a sibling.	Take him to reading time at the library or other outings where there are lots of children around.

What Your Child May Be Learning at Eighteen Months	What You Can Do to Help
LANGUAGE DEVELOPMENT	
Can say seven to 20 words and can name one body part.	Help her express her needs and wants in words. If she's scowling, say *"You look mad,"* or if she's pointing at an apple, say *"Do you want the apple?"* instead of just giving it to her.
INTELLECTUAL DEVELOPMENT	
Expects things to be in predictable places and things to happen at a routine time. He will know what comes next and what went before. For example, when you tell him it's dinnertime, he'll know that you'll be taking him to the bathroom to wash his hands.	Think about and plan the same routine each day. Let your child care provider know about your routines.
Memory is developing. She may continue to insist on having something you have taken away when earlier she would have quickly forgotten about it.	Be prepared to explain where things are or why she can't have something right now. **Be diligent in your supervision. Toddlers do not yet understand danger and quickly forget warnings you have given them. Ensure that all poisons and harmful cleaning solutions are locked out of your child's reach—she will remember where they are.**
May be able to follow simple directions, such as *"Bring me your doll,"* or *"Put the ball in the bucket."*	Give him small tasks, such as helping to clean up.
He will notice if you skip a page in a book.	Continue to share books with him and go back to the missed pages.
She continues to imitate what people do around her.	If you swear, don't be surprised to hear her curse too. Say only those things you would like your child to say.
He may love hiding and looking for things with you.	Include your child when you are looking for things you need to find.

Your Child at Two Years

At two years, your child's second molar teeth may be coming in, usually between 20 and 33 months. By now, she will be able to climb on furniture to reach windows and door handles. He may develop fears of things such as loud or unusual noises, clowns, and masks, and may have nightmares. Language will begin to take on a more important role in his life than it did at a younger age.

Children love to copy. Be a good example. Show your child how to do things by your actions.

What Your Child May Be Learning at Two Years	What You Can Do to Help
PHYSICAL DEVELOPMENT	
Carries a toy while walking, or pulls a toy behind him.	Let him help you with tasks in the yard or in the house when you need something small carried.
Runs, but may fall frequently. **Toddlers are also very quick-moving, so injury in traffic is a special consideration. When you are near cars, on a street, or in a parking lot, hold your child's hand. They are good at darting, running, and swerving, and can quickly escape from your supervision.**	Chase each other around the yard, with stops, starts, and sudden changes of direction to help develop muscle strength and control. Go up and down little hills, climb, slide, and roll to improve her balance and coordination. Have lightweight balls for kicking, throwing, and catching.
Can move his hand into the correct position before grabbing at something and may be able to unscrew lids or open doors by turning the knob.	Provide toys and materials, such as simple puzzles, stacking toys, and blocks, to help develop hand and wrist control. Make playdough and provide rollers or cookie cutters and plastic knives to shape and manipulate the dough.
Feeds herself with a spoon and uses a cup. Picks up tiny objects and crumbs.	Be patient—and be prepared to mop up spills.
May begin to dress himself with very simple, pull-on clothes.	Keep his clothes simple and easy to put on.
Climbs on furniture to reach windows and door handles. **Be aware that escape is now a possibility. Before your child begins trying to open outside doors, you may want to install a lock that she can't open.**	Give her large objects to climb on and into, such as cardboard boxes of varying sizes and shapes. Help her practise going up and down stairs.
Stacks a number of blocks.	Provide sand, water, or rice with containers of various sizes, funnels, buckets, and plastic cars and animals.
May be ready to start toilet training, or at least be interested in what you are doing in the bathroom.	See page 10 for information on "Getting Ready to Use the Toilet."

What Your Child May Be Learning at Two Years	What You Can Do to Help
SOCIAL AND EMOTIONAL DEVELOPMENT	
Enjoys being with other children, but may not yet be able to share, take turns, or play games with rules.	Introduce your child to a playmate so that she can begin to learn how to relate and communicate with her peers.
Likes to engage in parallel play—side-by-side play but not interacting—with other toddlers.	Supervise your child when he's playing with others. Try to prevent conflicts from occurring (see page 72 for information about challenging behaviours).
Observation skills increase. Copies the play of other children.	Talk with your child about what other children are doing in their play.
Does not realize that hitting or biting hurts (see page 73 for information on biting).	If your child is hurting another child by biting or hitting, explain that you cannot let her hurt anyone and redirect her activities.
Likes to imitate people around him and will do simple tasks that you are doing.	Let your child share in your activities by helping you clean the house or work in the yard. Give him child-size brooms, hoes, or other tools you also use.
May start to have tantrums and challenging behaviours.	Model kindness, patience, and sharing, and talk about how to solve conflicts peacefully. Talk about your own feelings: *"I'm sad we can't go to Grandma's house today."*
Will have growing confidence in being able to do things.	Try not to rush in and help to fix a problem right away—let your child master some things himself by making tasks simple. Praise your child often for her attempts to do things. If she has failed or done the wrong thing, focus your comments on the behaviour instead of the child: *"Throwing food on the floor makes a big mess"* instead of *"You are a bad girl."*
Understanding of self increases.	Talk about how his actions make other people feel. *"John is sad because you took his truck. He wanted to play with it too."*

LANGUAGE DEVELOPMENT

Knows the names of familiar objects and family members.	Use the correct names for people, places, and things.
Starts to say *"You," "Me,"* and *"I."*	Use the terms in your conversations.
Combines two to three words to make sentences, such as *"More milk."*	Chat with your child while you go about your daily activities.
Asks *"What's this?"* and *"Where's my…?"*	Be prepared to answer lots of questions. Name things clearly and the same way each time.
Says *"No"* and uses two-word negative phrases such as *"No want," "No go."*	Talk about what you are doing and feeling and what your child is doing and feeling.
Identifies body parts, foods, and clothing.	Play language games like *"Where is your ear?"*
Understands simple questions and commands, such as *"Come here." "Put Teddy in the stroller." "Where's your book?"*	Expand on the things your child says. If your child says *"Juice,"* you might say, *"Do you want to drink some juice?"*
Can go to another room and bring back an item that you request (unless she is distracted on the way).	Play games where you ask your child to bring things from one room to another: *"Can you find all of your teddies and bring them here?"*
Likes to read the same stories and hear the same rhymes over and over again.	Continue reading books and playing tapes and music.
Imitates sounds, particularly animal sounds.	Identify sounds with your child, such as *"barking dog, purring cat, singing birds, blowing horn."*

What Your Child May Be Learning at Two Years	What You Can Do to Help

INTELLECTUAL DEVELOPMENT

Begins to sort items by colour and shape.	Point out colours and shapes in conversation. *"Should we make square cookies or would you like circle cookies?"* *"You've chosen bright red socks to wear."*
Understands the meaning of *on top* or *under*, *inside* and *out*.	Provide toys that he can put together and take apart or toys that have pieces that fit together, such as simple puzzles, peg boards, and shape sorters.
Begins to understand ideas such as *more* or *one*: *"You can have one cookie."* or *"Do you want more milk?"*	Use these terms when talking with your child: *"This is one cookie, here are two cookies."* or *"Do you want more?"*
Is beginning to put ideas together and is able to plan her activities in advance, such as taking a toy to a friend's house to show him.	Talk about what you are going to do and describe plans for activities.
Remembers where objects are hidden over a long period of time.	**Make sure that all dangerous objects are put out of sight and out of reach—every time.**
Uses objects for their intended purpose; for example, he may put a telephone to his ear, comb his hair, and use a blanket to cover his doll.	Provide toys that encourage imaginary play, such as kitchen sets, dolls, dress-up clothes, telephones, and small tools. Be enthusiastic about everything he is learning to do.
Imagination is developing. May pretend to be a doctor to her dolls or may offer her mother an imaginary cup of tea.	Play with your child, but let her lead the way. Ask, *"What should we do with the red car?"* Give her crayons and large pieces of paper for scribbling. Provide finger paint and let your child spread it on a smooth surface.
Understands simple instructions and rules, such as *"We always drive with our seat belts on."*	Once you've established a rule, apply it each time—and follow it yourself.

Your Child's Development from Two Years to Three Years

The typical two-year-old is a walking, talking person with a mind of her own—one that changes frequently. During this year, your child may regularly move between being fiercely independent and being extremely clingy. She may sit in a stroller one minute and get out and walk the next. She may like broccoli on Monday and hate it on Friday. And she may know how to share her toys with one friend, but forget with another.

Before they're ready to share, toddlers need to learn about ownership. When your two-year-old holds her doll close to her chest and shouts *"Mine!"* it means she's starting to understand this concept. Gradually (and maybe not for another year or two) she will learn the joys of sharing.

Some children learn this skill earlier than others. You can help by showing your child what sharing looks like. You may say *"I'm eating this banana, but I'd like to share it with you"* as you break off a piece and give it to him. Or you might ask him to share when you know it will be easy for him. *"Would you please share your carrots with me?"*

Other skills your toddler starts to learn at this age include washing, dressing, feeding, and toileting. Two-year-olds also quickly develop physical skills— including becoming more stable on their feet. They need opportunities to practise these skills, and master them, in order to increase their self-esteem and encourage them to continue learning.

At this age your child is an active explorer, ready to try all kinds of new things. She explores by taking things apart, pushing in, pulling out, and doing things like filling and emptying containers. She enjoys playing imaginatively with trucks, dolls, and household items and, often, she will become completely absorbed in her play.

It's a good idea to give her some warning before you announce that playtime is over—or before you introduce any other significant change. This gives her time to change her focus and helps to reinforce her emerging understanding of time.

Remember that it's hard for children this age to cope with change of any kind, whether it's moving from playtime to nap time, having a new babysitter, or moving to a new house. You can help by talking about the change in advance, explaining why it's happening, and (where possible) reading him books about other children going through similar changes. Toddlers feel most secure when their lives and routines are predictable. So, when you're making a change, it's a good idea to maintain any rituals you've already established, such as those around bedtime and bath time.

As she tests her new skills and her new sense of independence, you may want to start setting clear, consistent limits and letting her know what kind of behaviour is okay and what is not. At the same time, you can encourage her further growth and development by letting her know that you're interested in what she's doing and by complimenting her efforts and achievements. She may also need to remember what it was like to be a baby. She may want you to rock her, cuddle her, hold her, and let her be your baby again. This is not regression. It's a natural part of development, and giving her time and attention refuels her for the serious business of learning that marks the third year of life.

What Your Child May Be Learning at Two-and-a-Half Years	What You Can Do to Help
PHYSICAL DEVELOPMENT	
Walks evenly forward, backward, and sideways. Runs with stops and starts.	Provide safe opportunities and space for running, jumping, climbing, and balancing.
Climbs well and jumps with both feet. **Climbing is fun, but with climbing comes falling. Be sure that the equipment your child plays on has a soft landing underneath: wood chips, mulch, sand, or other approved soft materials.**	Help and encourage your child to be active on playground equipment or any other safe climbing tools.
May help put things away, can carry things well, and pushes objects with good steering.	Involve your toddler in setting the table (with non-breakable dishes) or helping you with easy chores such as putting away clothes or toys.
Holds a crayon with her fingers rather than her fist. May be able to build a tower with eight blocks.	Provide puzzles, blocks, construction toys, water toys, large crayons, chalk, paint, etc.
Walks up and down stairs, with one foot on each step, holding the railing.	Keep reminding him that he must be careful on stairs and take his time.
Can walk on tiptoe for a few steps if you ask.	Play balancing games where you see who can stand on tiptoe the longest (and let them win often).
Can throw a large ball overhand.	Go outside and play catch with a large, soft ball.
Has often established whether he is right- or left-handed.	Accept whichever it is and provide crayons and paper so he can practise.
May be able to put her arms through large armholes, and may button one large button.	Look for clothes with easy-to-use buttons or snaps and encourage your child to dress herself as much as possible.
Unscrews lids and turns knobs.	Put toys in containers. **Think about safety when it comes to dangerous materials—things in jars or cupboards are no longer out of reach.**

SOCIAL AND EMOTIONAL DEVELOPMENT

May be coping better with separation from parents.	Talk about feelings. Respond to his needs. *"You are feeling sad because I am leaving for a while."*
Begins to be aware of differences between sexes, and can name his sex. May imitate what Mommy or Daddy does.	Don't be surprised if your toddler has very firm ideas about what mommies and daddies can do. Don't be shy about challenging some of them.

LANGUAGE DEVELOPMENT

Asks *"why?"* often.	Answer their questions in a simple way that they can understand. If you grow tired of a constant "why," sometimes ask them, *"Why do you think?"*
Can identify five body parts when asked.	Start adding new body part names once your child is able to regularly name ones he knows.
Can usually give her first and last name and may hold up fingers to show her age.	When meeting acquaintances, encourage her to introduce herself.
Refers to herself as *"I."*	Use these terms more often with your child, instead of saying, *"Mommy is going out"* start saying *"I am going out"* or *"We are going out."*
Can name one colour.	When getting dressed ask, *"What colour is your coat?"* And then tell him. When you see colours, name them for your child.

INTELLECTUAL DEVELOPMENT

Solves problems by trial and error.	Let your child try to work it out her way first. If she can't carry all of the toys she wants, let her try for awhile before asking if a bucket or box would help.
Understands time concepts such as *today, yesterday, tomorrow, before, after, now, soon.* And may be just beginning to understand time.	Use these words more often when talking with your child. *"I will be home after lunch"* or *"Remember what we did yesterday?"*, or *"Tomorrow we will go to the park."*
Can compare things, such as being bigger than another child, or having more cereal than his sister.	Provide puzzles that put things in order, such as smaller to bigger, or numbers.
Understands the concepts of *just one, some,* or *lots.*	Use these terms when talking together and point out when you see *"lots," "some,"* or *"one." "There are lots of kids here today. Yesterday there was only one."*

What Your Child May Be Learning at Two-and-a-Half Years	What You Can Do to Help
INTELLECTUAL DEVELOPMENT	
Understands action in pictures. Can respond to *"Who is running?"*	Talk about what you are reading and seeing in picture books.
Likes to play make-believe games.	Provide blocks, figures of people and animals, vehicles, houses, barns, and trains for building and imaginative play. Give your child dress-up clothes and props for make-believe play.
Still views the world as if he were the centre of everything. If he is describing something, he is assuming that you are seeing it too, even if you are talking to him on the phone: *"You see that, Mom? You like my picture?"*	Attend play groups so he will have an opportunity to be part of a group.
Talks about past experiences and future events.	Use special events like planning for Halloween or Grandma's birthday to emphasize the idea of time.
Can put together more complex puzzles.	Provide a felt board with felt shapes and figures to tell stories and make patterns. Talk about the story.

When drawing, he may make a circle for a head and a few lines for arms or legs. Nothing is to scale in artwork. Begins to create freely instead of copying.	Give your child art supplies, water, sand, playdough, and clay to use creatively. Include glue and collage materials of different shapes, colours, and textures.
	   Fold paper into airplanes and other objects. Creating crafts out of various supplies helps your child learn about textures and what different materials are like, such as what things will stick together and what won't.
	   Be sure to proudly display her artwork. This helps encourage more creativity and increases self-esteem.

Likes to be part of family activities.	Cook with your child and encourage her to help with food preparation. **Do not let your child play at the stove, since young children still do not understand the danger of burns.**
Can recognize changes in the tempo of music.	Play all kinds of music. Make musical instruments with your child and introduce him to real instruments like maracas, tambourines, and drums.

Your Three-Year-Old

Toddlers between two and three years of age are very mobile and can plan their activities themselves. You may find that your child is now able to push a chair over to the counter, climb up, open a cupboard, reach for a jar, and open it. Do not consider upper cupboards childproof—if your child wants something, she will think of a plan to get it.

What Your Child May Be Learning at Three Years	What You Can Do to Help
PHYSICAL DEVELOPMENT	
May be able to pedal a tricycle.	**Be sure your child wears an approved and well-fitting helmet whenever he is on a tricycle—even if he's just in the yard or the park. A helmet will reduce the severity of an injury.**
May have daytime control of bladder and bowel. Will be using the toilet fairly consistently, but may need help with wiping and will likely still be wet at night.	Praise their efforts at staying dry and using the toilet, and don't comment on any accidents.
Throws, catches, and kicks large balls.	Provide balls and beanbags and play throwing and catching games with your child.
Can usually dress and undress herself and put on her coat without help. Small buttons, laces, and zippers will still be too difficult for her and she will need your help.	Provide clothes, shoes, and boots with a variety of closures to practise lacing, zipping, buttoning, and tying.
Has the hand-eye coordination to attempt more complex activities.	Offer glue, wood, small hammers, and other carpentry supplies and supervise carefully.
SOCIAL AND EMOTIONAL DEVELOPMENT	
Plays with other children, sharing toys some of the time, but may still be possessive about his things.	Make sure that either you or another trusted adult is close by when children are together. You might need to help them or remind them of appropriate behaviour.
Friendships are brief, and your child may not seem to miss playmates from daycare or play groups, although she will speak of them fondly.	Encourage her to say "Hello" to playmates when she sees them.

What Your Child May Be Learning at Three Years	What You Can Do to Help
SOCIAL AND EMOTIONAL DEVELOPMENT	
Will have fewer tantrums, but may frequently fight with other children or siblings, often over a toy.	Help solve conflicts. *"Both of you want to use the tricycle. How can we solve this problem?"*
Often is rebellious, and gives orders like *"Go away."*	Try to be calm and not feel hurt when they test control of their world and independence.
Uses imaginary people and things in play or substitutes one object for another in play. Pretends he is someone else. A tea party may develop out of water, the cat, and a small dish. A pillowcase may become a cape or a stick may become a spear.	Join in the play and pretend along with your child. Encourage their imagination by asking questions that help them pretend more: *"Is our tea hot?" "Are you a superhero? Superheroes can run very fast!"* or *"Should we invite your dolls to eat with us too?"*
Likes to help with simple tasks. **Power tools or other tools that plug in and can be dangerous (such as glue guns) should be kept out of your toddler's reach. Your child loves to imitate you, and now has the fine motor skills needed to handle knobs, dials, or switches.**	When you are cleaning, give your child a damp cloth to help you with wiping. Many toddlers love playing with warm water and non-breakable dishes in the sink. Gathering leaves or helping to wash the car are also fun tasks.
Seeks approval.	Give both verbal and non-verbal approval. Smile and talk about what your child is doing.
Will understand others' feelings and will respond to them. If you are sad, she may give you a hug or say *"No be sad Mommy."*	Give more words for feelings, such as *disappointed*, *hurt*, *thrilled*, *excited*. Use these words to describe your own feelings and experiences.
May develop new fears as he becomes more aware of the world around him.	Listen to and accept his fears. Comfort and reassure your child. As at all times, cuddle, encourage, and show your child that you love him.
Her sense of ownership is developing. She may be upset about her things being given away.	Store clothing or toys that are outgrown. Give them away when she has forgotten about them.
Will have the language skills to be part of family and play groups.	Treat him with the same respect that you expect him to show to you and others. Model good manners. Say *"Please"* and *"Thank you"* to your child.

LANGUAGE DEVELOPMENT

Uses plurals (*dogs*), adjectives (*hot, little*), prepositions (*in, out, on*), pronouns (*I, me, he*).	When reading together, ask questions about the pictures in the book: *"Where do you think the boy is going?"*
Names several colours and can match colours.	Talk about colours when you're both getting dressed.
Is able to follow simple directions with two to three steps, such as *"Go to your room and get your red coat and bring it here to me."*	Read to your child frequently and provide plenty of books for him to look at on his own.
Uses four- to six-word sentences and has a vocabulary of 800 to 1000 words. May describe herself by her name: *"Chanel go to daycare now"* or *"Chanel hungry."*	Expand your child's sentences. If she says *"Mommy cook soup,"* say *"Yes, Mommy is cooking vegetable soup for dinner."*
Knows social words like *hello, please,* and *thank you.*	Play pretend social games with your child, such as: *"Who's come to visit us? Oh, it's Teddy! Hello Teddy, how are you?" "Thank you for coming to visit. Goodbye."*
Uses language to express needs and wishes and to direct others.	Play games using simple instructions that he can follow.
Asks many questions.	Have frequent conversations with your child and answer questions when she asks.
Can sing songs and recite finger plays and rhymes.	Make up silly rhymes, invent songs about what your child is doing, use silly words and phrases, and encourage your child to do the same. When brushing teeth or washing hands, sing a special song so that he learns to sing along.

Nutrition for Young Children

Food holds strong meanings for many of us. We eat certain foods for comfort, for a sense of community or tradition, for satisfaction, for nutrition, to grow and stay healthy. Parents play a big role in promoting healthy eating habits, which help children to grow and develop and to learn to enjoy a variety of foods.

Feeding Your Child

For children to eat and grow well, parents need to be sensitive to and respond to their children's messages about food and eating.

Helping toddlers learn how to eat and feed themselves can be trying times for parents. Avoid fighting about food. Nobody wins. To cope with feeding challenges, think of parents and children as having different "feeding responsibilities" or jobs.

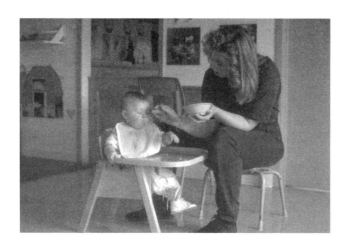

Young children know when they're hungry, and when they've had enough:

- You choose what to feed your child—breast milk or formula.
- You feed "on cue"—when your child is hungry. Stop when he signals that he's full by turning his head or pushing away.
- Your child chooses how fast and how much to drink or eat.

Young children need structure and routine around eating to feel secure:

- You offer a choice of healthy, age-appropriate foods.
- You offer meals and snacks at regular times.
- Your child chooses whether he eats and how much.

Sharing feeding responsibilities promotes attitudes and habits that form the basis for lifelong health.

Starting Solid Foods

At about six months your child will be ready for more than breast milk. You'll know your child is ready for solid food because he loves to watch you eat and may grab at your spoon or reach for your food. He can sit up with minimum support, close his mouth or turn his head when he is full. Children who start eating solid foods too early have more of a chance of developing food allergies. Before four to six months, a baby's tongue thrusts food out rather than moving it back with her tongue. By six months, your child is ready to experience the feel of different textures and tastes in his mouth. By seven months, all children should be eating "solid" foods.

It is exciting to start feeding your child solid foods. The first food that parents choose to start feeding their infants varies from culture to culture and from family to family. Offer foods least likely to trigger allergies: rice cereals, other single-grain infant cereals, carrots, squash, sweet potatoes, bananas, peaches, pears, beef, veal, lamb, chicken, or turkey. Foods such as iron-fortified infant cereals and meat are good choices to help prevent iron-deficiency and anemia.

When you start feeding your child solid foods, pick a time when she is alert and seems cheerful. She should have an appetite, but not be anxious for feeding. Seat her in a comfortable high chair, facing you. She may need help to sit upright. You may want to give her a second child-sized spoon to hold so that she isn't as likely to grab the feeding spoon.

Place a spoonful of iron-fortified rice cereal mixed with expressed breast milk, formula, or water near her lips. Give her time to look at it, to smell and taste it. Wait for her to open her mouth, then feed her and watch to see if she can close her lips over the spoon. If she takes the food, offer another spoonful. If she spits it out, wait a few minutes and try again. You can expect that most of the first "solid" food will end up on her bib, face, and high-chair tray. You are just getting your child used to eating—she doesn't need this food for nutrition yet. Learn your child's body language around food. When she's hungry, she may appear excited by waving her hands and kicking her feet when food is presented. She will lean forward and open her mouth. If she is not hungry, she may close her mouth and turn her head away.

PREVENT CHOKING

The greatest risk for choking is in children under three years of age. Their mouth muscles aren't developed enough to control hard or slippery foods. Foods that are round (grapes or peanuts) or very sticky (peanut butter) can cause choking. The airway of a young child is about the same diameter as a pencil.

Have your child teethe on a teething ring or a toy, not food. Even a baby can break off chunks of food and choke.

Make sure your toddler sits down while eating. Stay nearby to guard against choking; as well, eating is a social activity. Give foods in a form she can easily chew:

- Grate raw carrots; cook slightly or slice thinly hard vegetables such as broccoli; chop grapes, cherry tomatoes, and apples; and remove pits from cherries, apricots, peaches, and plums.
- Slice hot dogs or sausages lengthwise first and then into small pieces.

- Do not give children younger than three any globs of peanut butter, whole nuts, ice cubes, popcorn, chips (potato, corn, tortilla), whole marshmallows, hard candies, or jellybeans.

Training in Infant CPR will help you know what to do if your child does choke. For information on Infant CPR, talk to your public health nurse or local St. John Ambulance.

Toddler's Food Steps

	YOUR CHILD USUALLY:	YOUR CHILD IS READY FOR:
Around 6 months	• Sits up with very little help • Holds his head up • Watches for the spoon • Opens his mouth for the spoon • Closes lips over spoon • Moves solids around in his mouth • Turns his head to refuse food	• Solid food that is runny in texture, such as infant rice cereal mixed with breast milk, formula, or water; well mashed vegetables or fruit
6 to 9 months	• Moves food to sides of mouth • Munches • Bites off food • Grinds food with jaws • Picks up food in fingers or palms • Puts food in mouth • Closes lips around cup held by adult	• Thicker, lumpier food, e.g., mashed banana, avocado, or squash; minced or finely chopped meats, beans, lentils, tofu • Pieces of soft food as "finger food," e.g., soft and cooked vegetables and fruit without peels; toast strips, squares of bread, crackers, cooked rice, cooked pasta, "oat rings" cereal • Drinking from a sip cup
9 to 12 months	• Chews up and down • Uses thumb and finger to pick up small pieces of food • Cups hands around object • Twists and turns his hand with a spoon • Drop things from a high chair • Wants to sit at the family table and feed herself	• Family foods that are soft, cubed, or diced • Feeding herself messily—with fingers or spoon • Holding a sip cup
One to two years	• Uses a spoon and fork • Puts food in mouth and takes it out again • Dislikes foods he used to eat • Has less appetite after 18 months when she will be growing more slowly • Is easily distracted • May throw food to see how you will react	• Feeding herself messily with spoon or fork • Most family foods—note choking hazards
Two to three years	• Holds glass in hand • Spills a lot • Becomes fussy about food—may want the same foods over and over • Wants to do it herself • Dawdles over food • Wants food in certain shapes, whole foods • Eats a lot at times and a little at others • Prefers the texture of raw to cooked vegetables • Likes to help in kitchen	• Feeding independently if food is cut up • Most family foods—continue to watch for choking hazards

FEEDING NOTES

- Reduce chance of food allergies (Families with severe food allergies need to follow the advice of allergy specialists. See section on allergies, page 46.)
- Choose foods least likely to cause allergies
- Offer one food at a time
- Wait 4 to 7 days between new foods
- Feed solids with a spoon. Do not put solids in a bottle
- Wait until after 6 months to offer vegetables that may contain nitrates (beets, broccoli, carrots, cauliflower, green beans, spinach, turnips)

- Offer solid foods after breast or formula feeding
- Offer soft fruit (peach, pear, banana, kiwi, plum, melon)
- Offer minced or finely chopped meat and fish at 7 to 8 months
- Offer water in a sip cup
- Wait until after 9 to 10 months to offer milk products (milk, yogurt, cottage cheese, cheese slices, pasteurized cheese)

- Offer solid foods before breast or formula feeding
- Offer soft, cut-up foods, casseroles
- Offer whole milk occasionally when toddler is eating regular meals and a variety of solids
- Limit 100% fruit juice to 125 mL per day (in a cup)
- Wait until after 12 months to offer egg white and peanut butter (to reduce risk of allergies); and honey (to reduce risk of botulism)

- Limit 100% juice to 125 to 250 mL per day
- If weaned, offer whole milk in place of formula
- Braise, stew, or sauté meats to make them soft enough to chew
- Wait until after 2 years to offer fortified drinks such as soy milk, rice milk, or nut milk

- Limit 100% juice to 250 mL per day
- Preschoolers need 500 mL milk every day (after weaning)
- Gradually switch from whole milk to lower fat milk, e.g., 2%

You can get a copy of *Canada's Food Guide to Healthy Eating* from your local health unit, or from the Internet at www.hc-sc.gc.ca/hppb/nutrition/pube/foodguid/foodguide.html.

A TYPICAL DAY'S FOOD AMOUNTS
(the amount your toddler eats may vary from day to day)

- Feed solids 1 to 2 times per day
- Breast milk or iron-fortified formula 1000 to 1250 mL
- Start with 5 mL dry cereal mixed with liquid; and increase to 60 mL of prepared infant cereal and 60 mL vegetables or fruit at 6 to 9 months

- Feed solids 3 to 4 times per day
- Breast milk or iron-fortified formula 1000 to 1250 mL
- Infant cereal—60 to 125 mL
- Vegetables and fruit—60 to 125 mL
- Meat and alternatives—start with 5 mL and increase to 100 mL

- Feed solids 5 to 6 times per day
- Breast milk or formula—625 to 950 mL
- Infant cereal—60 to 125 mL
- Soft vegetables and fruit—125 to 250 mL
- Meat and alternatives—100 to 125 mL

- Feed 3 meals and 3 snacks
- Breast milk or whole milk
- Examples of child-size servings:
  Grain Products—5 or more per day
  ½ to 1 slice bread or piece of bannock
  15 to 30 g cold cereal
  75 to 175 mL hot cereal
  ¼ to ½ bagel, pita, bun, chapatti, or tortilla
  50 to 125 mL cooked pasta, rice, or congee (rice porridge)
  4 to 8 soda crackers
  Vegetables and Fruit—5 or more per day
  ½ to 1 medium-sized vegetable or fruit
  50 to 125 mL vegetables or fruit
  125 to 250 mL chopped salad
  50 to 125 mL juice
  Milk Products—2 to 3 per day
  500 mL milk or 2 servings (offered in small portions)
  25 to 50 g pasteurized cheese
  75 to 175 g yogurt
  Meat and Alternatives—2 to 3 per day
  25 to 50 mL meat, fish, or poultry
  1 egg
  25 to 125 mL beans or lentils
  50 to 100 g tofu

Learning About Food and Eating

Toddlers are learning to chew, swallow, and use a spoon. Young children approach food as they approach life—with a sense of curiosity. Food is to be explored, played with, tasted, and at times even eaten. To help your toddler learn to eat well, remember each of your "feeding jobs." You are responsible for the kind of food and how often it is presented and your child is responsible for if, and how much, he will eat. When he's eaten enough to be satisfied, his attention usually moves elsewhere. A toddler's appetite may not be predictable. He may want very little one day and gobble up his food the next—so don't encourage your child to eat more or less. This is *his* job. This is a good time to look at the foods your family eats and model healthy eating. Talk to older toddlers about the food choices you make and involve them in food preparation.

The "Toddler's Food Steps" chart (page 42) shows when your toddler may be ready to move to the next feeding step. Provide foods in a form that she can master, such as small, soft pieces, and start out with child-sized forks and spoons. It helps to schedule learning sessions when your child is fresh

and alert. Expecting a tired two-year-old to learn to use a fork after playing all day is not realistic. When your child is tired, give her "finger foods" that she can easily handle.

During the early weeks of "solid" feeding, your child is building eating skills. As she gets better at swallowing and chewing, she will need lumpier foods. Offer mashed foods for a short time so she develops the tongue movements she needs to deal with real food and doesn't become lazy about chewing. (Baby, Junior, and Toddler foods in jars are nutritious and convenient, especially when you are travelling. These foods can be expensive and may not give older toddlers enough of a chewing challenge.)

Don't expect her to like a new food the first time she tries it. Expect her to taste, but don't expect her to swallow. Young children do not readily accept new foods, unless they are sweet. It is normal for children to not accept a new food until it has been offered to them 12 to 15 times. Be patient and let your child explore and eat at her own pace. Eventually, she'll eat a variety of foods if she sees you and your family members doing the same thing.

Introduce a wide range of flavours and textures over time. See "What Do Toddlers Like to Eat?" (page 47). Serve "finger foods" that she can pick up for chewing and biting practice. Offer family food that has been cooked to soften it or mashed to make it easier to eat with few or no teeth. As your child eats more solids, she will drink less breast milk or formula. After she begins eating solids, introduce your child to as many different kinds of food as possible, one at a time (even foods you do not like).

When young toddlers try "finger foods" and foods with more texture, they sometimes gag. This is a normal part of learning to eat. A young child's gag reflex is very sensitive—and very effective in preventing choking. Remember that gagging is okay and healthy. Your toddler is learning how to eat without choking. If your child gags, don't panic. This could startle him and make him afraid to try new foods. Stay calm and reassure him by staying with him. You don't need to say anything.

Family Foods and Toddler Behaviour

By 12 months your toddler will be eating most of what the rest of the family is eating. Eat with her to show her how much you enjoy eating. Keep in mind that young children need more fat than adults do—for energy and for their brain development. Toddlers need higher-fat choices, such as whole milk, whole milk yogurt, full-fat cheese, avocado, margarine, butter, and salad dressing. As her growth is beginning to slow, her appetite may be unpredictable. She may eat a great deal one day and very little the next. This is a normal part of development, so you don't need to be too concerned. It's best to let your child decide how much to eat. Over a few days she will usually get all she needs.

Older toddlers may insist on having their milk in a certain cup, their food cut in certain shapes, or the same food every day for a week. This is common toddler behaviour. Toddlers often ask for the same food day after day. Be patient—this stage will pass. In the meantime, avoid short-order cooking. Catering to toddlers won't help them learn about, or learn to enjoy, a variety of foods. If your child asks for the same food over and over, as long as it is a healthy choice, try to include it with your regular planned meal. If beans are his favourite this week, just cook extra to keep on hand and put a little on his plate beside whatever else is being served. This way he is exposed to a variety of foods.

When you serve a new food, offer it along with something your child likes. Some children like "mini" versions of adult foods, such as pasta without the fancy sauce. Others like to dip their vegetables in salad dressing or their fruit in yogurt.

Older toddlers love to be part of the action and to learn about the food they eat:

- Explain why you make food choices. *"We're buying carrots because they're orange vegetables that give us some of the vitamins we need to stay healthy. Your father and I really like them steamed with a little butter."*

- Talk about why you buy—or won't buy—different foods. *"We will buy sugar-coated cereals as a treat when we go camping."*

- Have your child help you make meals and snacks. Show him how to mix fruit into his yogurt or to arrange pieces of banana on crackers. As one mother says, *"He enjoys putting his own cheese on a cracker. When he helps me make muffins, you can be sure he eats them all up."*

- Give your child healthy choices. *"Should we buy cucumbers or green peppers today?" "Do you want* *apple slices or pear slices in your yogurt?"* As another mother says, *"Before I make breakfast, I give him a choice between two items. But once he's made a choice, he can't change his mind."*

Watching Your Toddler Eat

Your child needs to explore food the same way he explores the rest of the world—with his eyes, hands, and mouth. This is an important part of learning. As he explores, he *will* make a mess because he doesn't have complete control of his hands and fingers. He may squeeze soft foods; he may miss his mouth and put food into his hair or ears. He may drop food on the floor by mistake—or on purpose to see how you react. Be patient and remember that "being neat" is not important to most toddlers. Give him small portions, let him eat at his own pace, have a wet washcloth or two nearby, and enjoy watching him learn. Serve meals in a place that is easy to clean and don't stress about the mess.

Are There Foods That I Shouldn't Give My Toddler?

In addition to foods that may cause toddlers to choke, some choices can be dangerous for young children. Wash your hands before handling food to avoid spreading germs in the kitchen. If you have any doubts about a food, milk, or formula, throw it out.

Bottles Heated in a Microwave Oven

Liquids can heat unevenly, possibly scalding your child's mouth. Glass bottles can get too hot and burn your or your child's hands. Plastic bottles may release chemicals into the hot liquid. It's safer to heat glass or plastic bottles of formula or milk in hot water. If you heat any food or drinks in a microwave, stir the contents well before serving to spread the heat more evenly.

Foods That Trigger Food Allergies

If there's a history of allergies, eczema, or asthma in your family, your child is at a higher risk of developing food allergies. Talk to your doctor, public health nurse, or a registered dietitian-nutritionist about what you can do to reduce the risk of your child developing a food allergy. Some things that help are exclusive breastfeeding for six months and careful introduction of solid foods (see below).

The following guide is for young children who have parents or brothers or sisters who have allergies, asthma, or eczema. These tips may help reduce the problems related to food allergies:

- Offer breast milk for at least one year to provide the best protection against allergies.
- Wait until after your child is 12 months old to introduce eggs, fish, milk products (e.g., whole milk, yogurt, cheese, cottage cheese, and ice cream), oranges, tomatoes, and strawberries.
- Wait until after two to three years to offer chocolate, shellfish, peanuts, peanut butter, nuts, and sesame seeds.

Too Much Fruit Juice or Sweet Drinks

Fruit juice, fruit-flavoured drinks, and pop are highly concentrated sources of sugar. Giving toddlers too many sweet drinks may lead to cavities, diarrhea, and poor weight gain. Offering juice before toddlers start on solid foods may result in the juice replacing the more nutritious and important breast milk or infant formula. Pieces of fruit may be a better choice, since fruit contains fibre.

Undercooked Meat and Eggs

Undercooked meat, poultry, fish, seafood, and eggs can cause food poisoning. Cook all meats until they are brown—NOT PINK—and the juices run clear.

HOW CAN I TELL IF MY CHILD IS ALLERGIC TO A NEW FOOD?

It's best to introduce new foods one at a time and wait four to seven days to see if your child has a reaction. *See a doctor immediately if your child has any of the following serious reactions:*

- swelling of the lips, face, or around the eyes that develops after eating a new food
- breathing problems
- vomiting (combined with other signs of allergy)

- hives (swollen, itchy patches of skin)

The following may also be signs of food allergies:

- bloating or an increase in gas or tummy pain
- diarrhea or mucusy bowel movement
- a rash that develops after eating the new food, including a persistent or severe diaper rash

- eczema (red, itchy skin)
- runny nose and eyes (with clear fluid, rather than mucus)
- unusual crankiness

If your child has any of these signs, stop feeding him the new food and talk to your doctor or dietitian-nutritionist (RDN). A dietitian can help you make sure your toddler is getting the nutrition he needs.

Fish should flake with a fork. Cook eggs until hard, with no soft or runny yolk.

Unpasteurized Milk, Cheese, and Juice

These foods may contain bacteria that can make children and adults very sick. Infants and toddlers are at the greatest risk and can become very ill or even die from exposure to these bacteria.

Honey if Your Toddler Is Under One Year

Honey may contain botulism spores that can make your child sick. These spores do not affect adults or older children. Cooked products containing honey (such as Graham wafers) do not pose the same risk.

Drinks High in Caffeine

Coffee, tea, and cola drinks contain too much caffeine for toddlers. Tea, coffee and cola also hinder iron absorption.

Raw Sprouts

Sprouts may carry bacteria if they are fertilized with manure.

What Do Toddlers Like to Eat?

Cool Ideas in a Bowl
- cold cereal with whole milk
- "oat rings" cereal and dried fruit pieces
- yogurt mixed with pieces of fruit or applesauce
- yogurt with crackers or roti
- fresh fruit pieces and yogurt for dipping
- rice and raisin pudding with milk
- soft tofu pudding

Cool Ideas on a Plate
- sandwiches made with egg salad, tuna salad, chicken salad, sliced tender meat, sliced or grated cheese
- cheese strips or small cubes (any kind) with whole grain bread or crackers or slices of apple or pear
- small muffins and orange wedges
- crackers or rice cakes thinly spread with cottage cheese or mashed avocado
- carrot or pumpkin bread thinly spread with cream cheese
- buttered toast spread with fruit purée

Hot Ideas
- hot cereal or congee (rice porridge) with whole milk
- bite-size pancakes or waffles topped with applesauce or other fruit
- soup made with milk; vegetable soup; split pea, lentil, or bean soup; fish chowder and bread sticks
- macaroni and cheese
- mini omelettes
- spaghetti with tomato or meat sauce
- meatballs with large noodles with an interesting shape
- pizza with lots of cheese
- soft tortillas or roti filled with beans or meat or eggs
- fish served in a bun
- baked beans and toast strips
- rice and meat with vegetables
- mild chili or lentils and rice

More Vegetable and Fruit Ideas
- soft, raw, or cooked vegetables with dip or hummus
- milk or yogurt shakes blended with fruit
- tomato or mixed vegetable juice
- grated carrots, beets, or cabbage in salad
- fresh fruit cut into wedges, with seeds and tough peels removed—apples, banana, berries, kiwi, melon, peaches, pears, plums
- cooked broccoli or cauliflower "trees" in mashed potatoes

How Much Food Does My Toddler Need?

Toddlers' appetites often vary widely and will change from day to day, so let your child decide how much to eat. One day she may eat very little food and the next day she may eat volumes. This is perfectly normal, since toddlers grow in spurts. The foods they like or dislike may change rapidly.

Serve a variety of healthy foods and do not focus on the amount she eats. Offer toddler-sized portions and give second helpings if your child wants more. As a rough guide, offer portions based on 15 mL (1 tbsp) per year of age. For example, offer a two-year-old 30 mL (2 tbsp) of meat, 30 mL (2 tbsp) of rice, 30 mL (2 tbsp) of broccoli, and 30 mL (2 tbsp) of applesauce at a meal.

See page 43 for child-sized servings, which range from 50% to 100% of the portion sizes listed in *Canada's Food Guide to Healthy Eating*.

What About Meal and Snack Times?

Because they have small stomachs, toddlers need to eat every two and a half to three hours. A normal day may include breakfast, snack, lunch, snack, dinner, and then bedtime snack. "Grazing"—allowing toddlers to eat and drink all day long—is a bad idea, since it provides a steady food supply to acid-producing bacteria that attack teeth and cause decay. If you serve foods that stick to teeth (like fruit leathers, cereals, and some crackers), offer them at mealtimes or at times when you can brush your toddler's teeth.

While toddlers want to be independent, they need the security of familiar things and events happening at regular times. They need you to establish structure in their lives and they enjoy having predictable meals at expected times. Children need to learn to eat at routine times—when they're hungry, not when they're bored or needing comfort. Don't

RELY ON YOUR CHILD'S EATING CUES

Letting your child decide for himself whether to eat, and how much to eat, gives him a chance to explore and develop healthy eating and social skills. It can also take some of the pressure off you, as a parent, when you know there are certain things you shouldn't try to control. Studies show that parents who rely on children's cues regarding hunger and fullness have taller, leaner toddlers who eat more than others at the same age.

Saying *"No"* to food is a way of showing independence. If your toddler won't eat, try to be calm and let him make this decision for himself. Missing one meal or snack will not hurt his health. Wait until the next regular meal or snack to offer him more food.

Choosing whether to eat is your child's job. Never force him to eat or punish him for not eating. Don't use dessert as a bribe to eat the rest of the meal. Don't use food for comfort—instead, give your toddler attention and affection.

Sometimes, children refuse to eat for reasons other than being full. If you play detective, you may discover why your child is not eating. Exploring some of the following options could help:

• Is she too excited, tired, upset, distracted, or sick to eat? Try to schedule a rest or a calm activity before meals.
• Is he too full? Check the amount of juice or milk he's drinking. More than 250 mL (1 cup) of juice and more than 550 to

750 mL (2–3 cups) of milk a day can leave little room for other food. To avoid this problem, use water as a thirst quencher and show your toddler that you enjoy drinking water too.
• Ask an older toddler why she doesn't want to eat. Some foods may be touching each other, or she may not like a strange texture. Children's taste buds are more sensitive than those of adults, and they are less able to tolerate strong flavours.
• Maybe he doesn't like the taste. You don't like all foods; neither will your child. Be matter-of-fact. *"That's okay, you don't have to eat it. You might not like this until you are older."*

use food as a way to change their behaviour. If you use food to bribe your child to behave, he will view food as a reward rather than eating to satisfy hunger. Giving him a cookie to keep him occupied while you are on the phone or driving won't help him to learn the right reasons for eating, which should be hunger and nutrition.

Eating together makes meals a special and pleasant time for families. It also encourages toddlers to eat what the rest of the family is eating. Try to establish having at least one meal a day together as a family to share time with each other and develop closeness. Memories of family times often involve food: a special birthday cake, where you all sat at the table, favourite meals, or routines of "who did what" at dinner time.

Reduce distractions and make the meal enjoyable by turning off the TV, keeping toys away from the table, and talking with your family about the day's activities. Let your toddler be messy with food—this is part of learning to eat—and don't rush feeding.

Toddlers have difficulty staying still for an extended period of time, but you can expect them to stay at the table for at least 10 minutes. Being comfortable and able to reach things will make your child more willing to stay put until the end of the meal. When mealtime is over, everyone leaves the table. (See page 101 for information on choosing a high chair, booster, or hook-on seat for your child.)

Does My Toddler Need Vitamin-Mineral Supplements?

Breastfed infants need vitamin D drops from birth until they are drinking 500 mL of formula or whole milk each day. Health Canada recommends vitamin D supplements (10 micrograms per day) for all breastfed full-term infants. For infants living in northern communities, 20 micrograms per day of vitamin D is recommended.

Food contains the energy and most of the vitamins and minerals your child needs. If your toddler is eating a variety of foods from all the food groups, is growing well and appears healthy, she probably doesn't need extra vitamins or minerals.

If your child isn't eating well, speak to your **doctor or dietitian-nutritionist.** Iron deficiency is of special concern for toddler growth and brain development. Meat and alternatives are good sources of iron. So are grain products eaten with a source of vitamin C, such as oranges or juice with vitamin C added.

If you give your child a supplement ...
Continue to follow the *Food Guide.* Choose a supplement approved for toddlers. Use a liquid supplement until your child has her molar teeth in and is chewing well. Sugar-free chewables are a good choice. Offer supplements along with a meal and brush their teeth afterwards. Don't refer to supplements as candy or treats and keep them out of children's reach. Don't give cod-liver oil to toddlers—it is too high in vitamin A. Overdoses of vitamins A or D or iron can be toxic.

Vegetarian Food Choices

If you are vegetarian and want your toddler to follow this pattern, select foods carefully to meet her nutrition needs. Offer vegetarian choices from each group of *Canada's Food Guide to Healthy Eating* to help your toddler get the foods she needs to grow and develop.

Shortfalls in nutrition can occur if you severely restrict food choices, e.g., offering no milk products or meat and alternatives. Nutrition shortfalls can affect growth and development.

Offer your vegan toddler:
- Breast milk or soy-based formula until two years of age.
- Fortified soy milk and calcium-set tofu as an alternative to cow's milk. (Check ingredient lists for calcium).
- Meat alternatives such as tofu, soy, or veggie "meats" such as veggie burgers, beans, peas, lentils, nut and seed butters. Thin nut or seed butters with juice or other liquids to help her swallow them without choking.
- High-energy foods including tofu, avocado, margarine, nut and seed butters, and soy cheeses.

If you have questions or concerns about vegetarian or vegan choices, contact Dial-a-Dietitian at 1-800-667-3438, or the nutritionist at your local health unit.

A Sample Day's Menu for a Toddler

The following menu shows how Jasmine's parents make sure she gets all the nutrition she needs in a typical day. Jasmine is almost two years old. She spends time in daycare and insists on feeding herself, just like the older children. This menu may help you plan for your own toddler.

Toddler Table Manners

Have age-related expectations of table manners for your child. Start small and gradually build manners as your child gets older and more capable of understanding what it is she's doing and why. Remember that you want the table to be a relaxed and pleasant place to be, so take the pressure off your toddler. It's a good idea to focus on telling her what you want—

	FOOD SERVED	SERVING SIZE	GRAIN PRODUCTS	VEGETABLES AND FRUIT	MILK PRODUCTS	MEAT AND ALTERNATIVES
7:30 Breakfast	Orange juice	125 mL		1		
	Scrambled egg	1				1
	Toast with margarine	½ slice	1			
	Whole milk	125 mL			1	
9:30 Snack	Bran muffin	½	1			
	Cheese slice	25 g			1	
12:00 Lunch	Strips of cold roast beef	25 g				1
	Pasta salad with dressing	50 mL	1			
	Cold cooked peas	50 mL		1		
	Whole milk	60 mL			½	
	Fruit cocktail	50 mL		1		
	Oatmeal cookie	1	1			
2:30	Water after her nap					
3:00 Snack	Banana	½		1		
	Melba toast with cream cheese	2	½			
5:00 Dinner	Steamed rice	50 mL	1			
	Curried lamb	25 g				1
	Cooked carrot coins with margarine	50 mL		1		
	Yogurt	75 g			1	
	Water					
7:30 Bedtime Snack	Corn flakes	15 g	1			
	Whole milk	60 mL			½	
	Apple juice	50 mL		1		
	Total number of servings		6½	6	4	3

instead of what you don't want. Reminders of table manners, such as *"Try to use your fork for the noodles like I do"* or *"Let's keep the food on the plate so it stays clean"* work much better than *"Stop that now or else leave the table!"*

Toddlers are learning the rules about eating, and you can help by modelling appropriate mealtime behaviour. And, since toddlers love to copy the big kids, older siblings can play a valuable role by showing the younger ones acceptable table manners.

One parent describes how she encourages her child to eat at the table: *"Pick the chair that you want to sit in. There, you sit in that one and I'll sit beside you in this one."* When a spill occurs, instead of scolding she encourages her child to help in the cleanup: *"Your milk fell over. That's okay. Here's a cloth to clean up the table. We'll clean up the floor later."* As in other areas, it's important to set clear, understandable limits. For example, you may want to make it clear that throwing food is not acceptable by calmly stating *"We don't throw food. The next time will mean the meal is over."* Follow through. Toddlers learn quickly.

Make sure that your toddler can understand what it is you are expecting of him. Saying *"Don't eat the green part of the watermelon"* to an 18-month-old will fail, since he doesn't know what green means. Instead, say *"Eat this part here, not that part,"* or better yet, give him only the red section. *"Stop acting like that"* is another example of a request doomed to failure. Instead, be specific. Saying *"Stop dropping your food on the floor"* is more likely to get the response you want.

Other Helpful Comments at Mealtime

- *"This is called a burrito. Johnny's mother makes them. I thought you might like it."*
- *"Please sit properly so that we can enjoy your company."*
- *"It's okay if you don't want to eat any peas—would you like some more potatoes?"*
- *"Are you finished? Okay. Snack time will be in a couple of hours."*
- *"Oh, you don't want to swallow that bite? Here is a tissue for you to politely put it in the garbage."*

Eating Out with Your Toddler

The best way to teach your child how to act in a restaurant is to take her out to eat once in a while.

Family restaurants are a good choice. Many ethnic restaurants are also family-friendly. You may be tempted to take your child to a fast food restaurant, since toddlers often have difficulty waiting. There are also lots of healthy foods that can be served quickly, including sushi (without raw fish), wraps, soups, salads, pasta, Asian rice bowls, and sandwiches. If you buy food at a drive-through restaurant, avoid eating "on the run" from a bag as you drive. Children need to learn to pay attention to what is going into their bodies and to recognize the sensation of fullness—so sit down, slow down, and enjoy every bite of the meal.

You can make a meal out more enjoyable if you take along things like toys, food, colouring books, and crayons that your toddler likes. You may also want to carry a plastic cloth to put under the high chair if your child tends to be particularly messy.

If your child doesn't like any of the meals on the menu, consider ordering a side dish like tiny noodles, beans, blueberries, or cut-up fruit. Many restaurants are willing to make a small bowl of pasta without sauce for toddlers.

After you order, take a walk or provide some other distraction such as a toy or story. This will make it easier for your toddler to wait for the food to arrive. If your toddler is unable to sit quietly and is bothering the other diners, leave as soon as possible. You may choose to get the meal "to go" or to have one person take the child out for a walk while the other eats.

Life on the Go

If you aren't at home for feeding times, take along nutritious and tidy snacks such as dry cereal, cheese and crackers, cut-up fruit such as apple or pear, or cut-up vegetables. Save snacks that can be messy (e.g., yogurt or soup) for times at home or when your child can sit at a table.

You may also want to carry plastic forks, knives, and spoons and some wet wipes in a plastic bag in your backpack, purse, or the glove box of your car. That way, you'll always be prepared for snack time.

Invest in small containers with tight-fitting lids so that you can easily take along snacks without risk of spills. A small plastic drink container with a collapsible spout is handy for milk or water.

What About My Child's Weight and Height?

Like adults, healthy children come in various shapes and sizes. Young toddlers often appear chubby, especially before they are walking. When they begin to be more active, the extra plumpness will usually fade away. If you are worried about your child being larger or smaller than you may be expecting, ask yourself the following questions:

Am I offering her wholesome foods?

Is physical activity a regular part of our day?

Does she seem healthy, happy, active, and alert?

Are most of the people in our family large or small?

If you continue to be concerned, talk to your doctor, public health nurse, or dietitian-nutritionist. They can weigh and measure your child and record her pattern of growth over time. While growth charts provide a way to "map" your child's growth, these are not targets or ideals. (Most height/weight charts reflect the growth patterns of bottle-fed infants. Breastfed infants tend to be leaner than formula-fed infants and gain weight more slowly, especially after six months. Their rates of increase in length and head circumference are about the same.)

Knowing your child is tall or short, thin or plump is not as important as establishing lifelong healthy eating and exercise habits (see page 82 for information on getting active and having fun with your child). Even if your toddler looks heavier than others, allow her to eat and grow naturally. Most children know how much food they need. Children should not be put on "diets." Studies have shown that toddlers are heavier when their parents control what they eat.

What About Weaning?

The Canadian Paediatric Society recommends that breastfeeding continue for up to two years of age and beyond. You and your child decide when it's best for you to stop. Breastfeeding a toddler provides him with more than milk. It is an important source of comfort, cuddling, and closeness with you. Weaning will change this—so expect him to want more of your attention, love, and affection during this time. He may satisfy his sucking needs by sucking his thumb, a soother, or stuffed animals or blankets. You may be looking forward to an immediate decrease in your child's demands on your time and energy when you stop nursing, but this will most likely not be the case. You may find that you are spending more time holding, comforting, and settling your toddler. If your child seems to be clinging even more, don't worry—this is a passing phase, and will decrease when he learns new ways to comfort himself and is reassured that you are not deserting him.

If your child is younger than about nine months, weaning will mean replacing breastfeeding with bottles of expressed breast milk or formula. Ask your doctor or the nutritionist at your health unit which formula is best for your toddler. If your child is between nine months and one year old and drinking well from a cup, you can bypass the bottle altogether by serving expressed breast milk, formula, or whole milk in a sip cup.

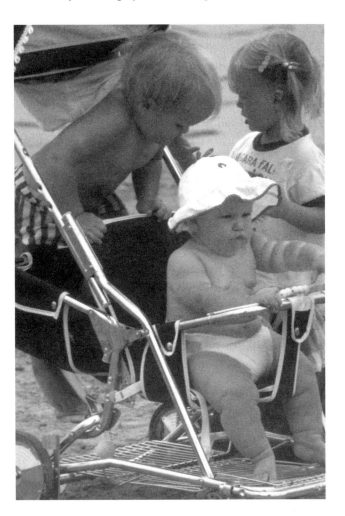

Gradual Weaning

Gradual weaning is usually the best method for both mother and child because it gives you both time to adjust to your changing relationship. A slow decrease in nursing also gives your breasts a chance to naturally reduce the amount of milk produced, and bypasses potential milk engorgement and the potential for mastitis or breast abscess. If you stop suddenly, your child may also be confused or distressed at the sudden lack of closeness he would have normally had on a regular basis.

Pick your time carefully. Don't begin weaning if your child is going through another stressful event in his life, such as beginning daycare, meeting a new sibling, or feeling ill or out of sorts in any way. When you are ready to begin weaning, start slowly by skipping one feeding every two days. Pick the least favourite or least-needed feeding—often the midday feeding—to eliminate first. You can either replace the feeding with formula or, if your child is over six months, give drinks and food instead. Your child probably won't need as many feedings as he did when breastfeeding, so don't worry if he's not hungry as often. It is useful to anticipate feeding times and offer substitutions and distractions instead of the breast. If one of the feedings is more out of habit than nutritional need, you can try distracting your child by changing your routine at that time. Instead of being in the house at the two o'clock feeding time, give him a snack or drink and go to the park for a walk. Once you have replaced one feeding with

a substitute, wait two or three days, or until you are both ready, and then replace another of the least favourite feeding times.

Continue in this way until you are down to the number of feedings a day you are happy with. This may be none at all, or may be only at bedtime or first thing in the morning. At this point you can breastfeed just enough to relieve the fullness in your breasts. Milk production may be very low and may gradually cease. When you are ready to halt the bedtime breastfeeding, it may work best to have your partner or another family member put your child to bed while you are out of the house.

Nursing is a natural way of delaying your period, so if you have not already begun menstruation, you will most likely begin now. Remember that breastfeeding is not a good form of birth control. You can become pregnant while breastfeeding, even if you are not menstruating. Your periods may be irregular for the first few months after weaning, and you may notice that some milk continues to be produced for weeks or even months after weaning is completed.

Can I Continue Breastfeeding?

- **If I'm pregnant again:** Yes. In a normal pregnancy there is no reason for you to stop nursing. You will be eating for more than two at this time, so be sure to get enough nutrition for your unborn child, your nursing toddler, and yourself.
- **If I'm returning to work:** Yes. You will still be able to nurse your child before you leave and again when you see her after work. Many workplaces support the nursing mother's need for a private place where breast milk can be expressed, and with a little planning you will be able to store this milk and have it given to your child the next day at daycare. See the *Baby's Best Chance* sections on breastfeeding and working, and expressing and storing breast milk.
- **If I'm prescribed medication:** There are few medications that require weaning, and often substitutes can be found. Always inform your doctor that you are breastfeeding if a medication is prescribed.
- **When my child has teeth:** Yes. You may be concerned about being bitten. If your child accidentally nips you while nursing, your natural

reaction of yelping would be appropriate. It gives your child immediate feedback that biting is not pleasant and should not be repeated. If your child continues to bite you, talk to a lactation consultant.

- **If my child or I go into hospital:** This would be an especially poor time to wean your child. Stress and fear are highest in these situations; your child needs your attention and closeness, and would benefit from the immune factors found in your milk.
- **If I develop mastitis (breast infection):** Milk from a breast with mastitis is not bad for your child. In fact, it is helpful to continue breast-feeding with mastitis, as the breast is emptied regularly and pain is decreased.

Breastfeeding Your Older Toddler

If you feel reluctant to nurse your older child in public due to the comments or reactions of others, be assured that you are not harming your child and that breastfeeding is a normal and healthy activity. In order to avoid tooth decay from the high sugar content of breast milk, remember to brush your child's teeth after nursing at bedtime. In order to make nursing as comfortable as possible, there are ways of planning ahead and reducing the pressure on yourself and your child.

- Some children are willing and able to accept limits on when and where they can nurse. Your child may be happy with the rule that he can nurse only at home.
- Plan for private places to nurse your child—in the car before going into the mall, or in the bedroom at friends' homes, and in change rooms at stores. These are all suitable spots for a little quiet time with your child.
- Have distractions and substitutes ready and at hand when you are out. Snacks, toys, and other drinks may be enough to hold off your child until you are in a private place.

- If you still hear comments from strangers such as, *"How long are you planning on nursing?"* you can always come back with replies such as, *"Only a few more minutes"* or *"We're in the middle of weaning right now."*

Weaning Your Toddler from the Bottle

If your toddler drinks from a bottle frequently—using it for comfort rather than nutrition—he may be at risk for tooth decay. He's also at risk if he sips anything other than water from a bottle, sip cup, or drinking box frequently during the day or while falling asleep. Remember to clean his teeth before bedtime.

You can reduce the risk by introducing a sip cup between the ages of six and 12 months and gradually phasing out your toddler's bottle. He may be very attached to it, so it's best to start weaning when he's not facing other changes or dealing with stressful situations.

Ways to Help Make the Weaning Process Easier:
- Offer milk in sip cups at meal and snack times only.
- If you offer bottles between meals and snacks, fill them with water.
- If your child is very attached to having milk in his bottle, gradually decrease the amount of milk you use. Then substitute water and gradually decrease the number of bottles you offer each day.
- Encourage your toddler to sit down with you when he has a bottle, rather than walking around with it.
- Limit the number of places your child is allowed to be while drinking a bottle.
- Show your child his teeth in a mirror and talk about the importance of taking care of them.
- Your toddler may miss having his bottle for comfort. Try to understand as he finds other comfort objects, such as a soother, thumb, blanket, or teddy during this time.

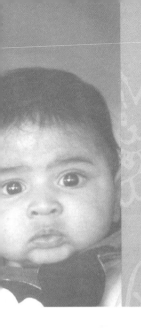

CHAPTER 3

Your Child's Health

Very young children can begin learning how to stay healthy by eating a variety of nutritious foods and getting plenty of rest and exercise. As a parent, you can help by teaching your child how to keep himself safe, how to wash his hands, and how to brush his teeth. Remember: when your child develops healthy habits, he's likely to keep them for the rest of his life. That means fewer illnesses, fewer trips to the doctor, and overall, a better quality of life.

Health care begins with hand washing—one of the most effective ways to prevent the spread of germs. You can protect your toddler's health by teaching proper hand washing and encouraging him to do it often. Use plain soap and wash under warm, running water for at least 15 seconds or about the length of time it takes to sing the happy birthday song. (Keep water temperature at 49°C/120°F or less to avoid burns.) And make sure your toddler watches you wash your own hands. When he sees you doing it regularly after using the bathroom and before eating or handling food, he'll want to do the same thing.

did you know?

 Antibacterial soap is not recommended. Plain soap and warm, running water are all you need to get your hands clean.

Looking After Your Child's Teeth

Even though "baby" or first teeth are replaced by permanent teeth, these first teeth are very important because they:

- Help your toddler to eat well.
- Play an important role when your child is learning how to speak.
- Help in jaw development and guide the permanent teeth into their proper position.
- Help your child to look good.

You have most likely already been cleaning your child's mouth with a clean wet cloth or soft toothbrush since soon after birth. This is a good start toward a lifetime of healthy teeth.

did you know?

It is important to brush baby teeth because the tooth buds for permanent teeth are growing underneath.

Diet and Tooth Decay

How often food is eaten and how long it stays on the teeth are two of the most important influences on tooth decay. Your child's teeth can develop decay from the first day they appear. Breast milk, cow's milk, formula, fruit juice, and soft drinks all contain sugars that can cause tooth decay. This will happen if the foods are frequently left in contact with teeth or gums for long periods of time. Allowing a child to have a bottle or sip cup during the day for long periods, or giving a bottle or prolonged breastfeeding during sleep times (naps and overnight), can cause decay in a child's teeth. Decay starts along the gum line behind the top front teeth, which makes it hard to see. Decay then spreads to the front of these teeth and can often affect all the teeth.

How Tooth Decay Can Be Prevented:

- Give plain water in sleep-time bottles. If you are having difficulty getting your toddler to settle without milk, try decreasing the amount of milk in the bottle at each nap, replacing it with water. Don't stop halfway, as watered-down milk can still cause cavities. This change to water only is best done over a short time such as one week. A good way of looking at bottle use is to think: if the bottle is given for feeding, use milk; if it's given for comfort, it should contain water.
- Give plain water instead of sweetened drinks when your child is thirsty. More water is needed during hot weather. Children drinking breast milk, formula, or milk and eating fruits and vegetables don't need juice. Try to avoid sweetened drinks like pop, Kool-Aid, and punches.
- Have cups ready, since your child may want to drink from a cup starting at about six to nine months of age.
- Discourage your toddler from constant sipping or snacking. Constant nibbling or sipping provides a steady supply of food for the bacteria that cause tooth decay. To avoid this, offer your toddler healthy snacks at regular times and limit the time he spends with a bottle or sip cup. One method of reducing the time spent with a sip cup or bottle is to make the rule that he must sit at the table to drink. Your child's desire to roam will naturally make his drinking times shorter.
- Brush your toddler's teeth immediately after he's eaten dried fruit (such as raisins or fruit leather), candy, or other foods that stick to teeth.

What About Fluoride?

Fluoride is an effective and inexpensive way to make tooth enamel stronger and more resistant to decay. Most large cities in Canada add a small amount of fluoride to the drinking water in order to prevent tooth decay in all age groups. If you are not sure if your community water is fluoridated, call your local health unit.

All children will benefit from using fluoride toothpaste, whether they are drinking fluoridated water or not. Careful use of fluoride toothpaste is one of the best ways to prevent tooth decay. Follow these simple steps:

- Check the toothpaste package to make sure that it contains fluoride. Some "baby toothpastes" do not contain fluoride.
- When your child's teeth appear, put a smear of toothpaste on a clean wet cloth or baby toothbrush and wipe or brush twice a day, in the morning and before putting your child to bed at night.
- As your child gets older and back teeth appear, gradually increase the amount of fluoride toothpaste to a pea-sized amount on a baby toothbrush.

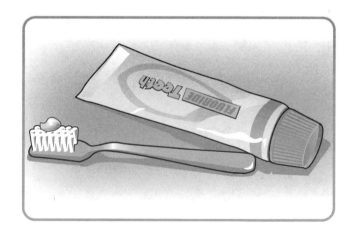

Most children will get enough fluoride from using fluoride toothpaste twice a day. Some children who are at high risk for tooth decay may need additional fluoride. Talk to your dentist or local health unit if you are concerned that your child may be at high risk for decay.

Brushing Your Child's Teeth

Regular mouth care will massage the gums and help ease your child's teething discomfort. Dentists recommend that parents brush their children's teeth for them until they are at least six years old, since toddlers are unable to clean their own teeth thoroughly.

Follow these steps to set a positive tone and to get your child's cooperation with dental care:

- Be a positive role model and practise good dental care yourself by brushing your own teeth twice a day. This is important for two reasons. First, toddlers will follow you and learn from you. Second, be aware that you can pass on decay-causing germs to your child by tasting her food, kissing her, or licking her soothers.
- Plan for teeth brushing when your child is not tired or hungry, as she will be better able to help you brush her teeth.
- Have your child sit comfortably in your lap, or lie comfortably on a change table, or the floor.

If using the lying down position, be sure that your child does not choke. Talk or sing to your child while you brush. As your child grows, get a stable stool for use when standing in front of the sink.

- Have a good look into your child's mouth while brushing. Support her neck or chin and check that you have enough light to see well.
- Gently brush the surface of your child's teeth with a baby or child's toothbrush with a smear (no larger than pea size) of fluoride toothpaste, twice a day. Also brush her tongue to remove bacteria that forms there.
- Make a game of brushing her teeth, or sing a silly song that relates to clean teeth. It's easy to make one up that rhymes with "Twinkle, Twinkle, Little Star."
- Make time for frequent spitting and swallowing. Toddlers have more saliva than adults and need regular breaks to swallow.

Teething

Once teething begins, it continues almost uninterrupted for about two years. Although each child has his own schedule for cutting teeth, you can expect the first tooth to come through at about six months of age (see the chart on this page for details). By about three

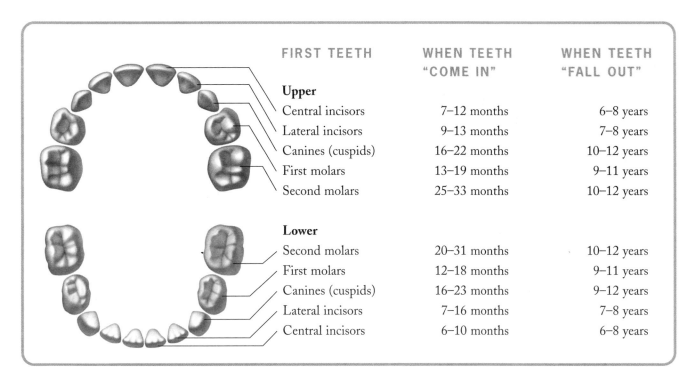

FIRST TEETH	WHEN TEETH "COME IN"	WHEN TEETH "FALL OUT"
Upper		
Central incisors	7–12 months	6–8 years
Lateral incisors	9–13 months	7–8 years
Canines (cuspids)	16–22 months	10–12 years
First molars	13–19 months	9–11 years
Second molars	25–33 months	10–12 years
Lower		
Second molars	20–31 months	10–12 years
First molars	12–18 months	9–11 years
Canines (cuspids)	16–23 months	9–12 years
Lateral incisors	7–16 months	7–8 years
Central incisors	6–10 months	6–8 years

years of age your child should have 20 teeth, 10 on the top and 10 on the bottom. Some children seem to have no problem with teething, while others may be fussy, uncomfortable, or off their food. Be prepared for extra drooling (bibs help) and chewing (provide soft, clean toys or teething rings) while teething.

Tips on Relieving Sore or Tender Gums

- Give your child a clean, chilled teething ring to chew on. Check teething rings frequently to see that they are in good condition. If it is cracked or worn, throw it away. Teething cookies, biscuits, or other foods are not a good choice since they contain sugar that can lead to tooth decay. Also, a child can break off pieces of food and choke.
- Teething gels or ointment should be used only on the advice of your doctor or dentist.
- Extra love and patience will help your child through the teething process.

Soothers

Soothers are sometimes given to infants at rest and sleep times or at other times when the child has been fed but still wants to continue sucking. Using a soother or pacifier is thought to be better than letting a child suck his thumb or fingers, since it is easier to break a soother habit when he gets older. Soothers are not recommended for use once the complete set of baby teeth has come in, usually by about three years of age. If your toddler is still regularly using a soother at that time, it may affect normal speech, mouth, and jaw development.

If your child is using a soother, make sure it is a one-piece design. You should:

- Examine the soother often—if it is sticky, cracked, or torn, throw it away. Give a strong tug on the nipple to make sure it is firmly attached to the shield. As teeth begin to come in, the soother will often be used as a teething tool and can easily be torn, which presents a choking hazard for your child.
- Never dip the soother into honey, syrup, or any other sweetener, since this can lead to tooth decay. Unpasteurized sweeteners may also put your child at risk for disease.
- Give your child a clean soother that has been washed in warm water. Don't wet or clean the

soother in your own mouth, since this can infect your child with germs that cause tooth decay.
- For safety reasons, never tie the soother around your child's neck or attach it to his clothes with a cord.

did you know?

Some new research links regular use of soothers with frequent ear infections. Only use them for short periods of time. Stop using them as early as possible in the first few years of life.

It may be time to wean your child off the soother if:

- He's spending the majority of the day with the soother in his mouth.
- The soother is getting in the way of his activities or development. He is pointing to an object instead of asking for it, or not talking with other children because of the soother.
- Your child is not developing other ways of comforting or calming himself.
- Your dentist recommends that the soother be taken away due to problems with the development of your child's teeth and jaw.

When your child has a soother in his mouth, he has a "plug" or "stopper" blocking his ability to use words and talk and to use new coping skills. If your child is turning to the soother whenever he's facing a frustrating or challenging task or situation, he is missing an opportunity to develop new ways of working through frustration. If your child is crying because he can't solve a puzzle, a soother may not be the best tool to use to stop the crying. Instead, talk with him and try to understand what it is he wants and why. At an early age he will have limited verbal skills and may only be able to point and grunt, but he is communicating with you. Try to help him find ways of learning the skills he is finding hard, rather than letting him go to the comfort of a soother right away.

Around their third birthday, many toddlers will lose or reduce their interest in sucking on a soother or thumb. If your child is not losing interest, or you want to end the soother use earlier, try to:

- Begin to get rid of a soother when life is stable for your child, not during a time of change, such as a new daycare or an illness.
- Limit where and when he can have the soother, slowly getting it down to one place at one time. This often ends up being during naps or bedtime. Once your child is asleep, gently remove the soother from his mouth.
- Provide substitutes for comfort instead of the soother. Give extra hugs, songs, and attention whenever your child starts to want the soother.
- Make sure your child is well fed and rested, making it easier for him to cope with change and stress.
- Reinforce positive behaviour with stars on a chart or the promise of a special treat or outing. A phone call to Grandpa or Auntie to report on how long the soother has been put away may be a positive event.

When You Visit the Dentist

If you have a concern about your child's teeth—discoloured teeth or spots on your child's teeth may indicate a problem—make an appointment to see your dentist even if your child has only a few teeth. On the first dental visit, expect the dentist to have a look in your child's mouth and to provide information on nutrition, fluoride, and ways to care for her teeth. Your child may be eligible for the Healthy Kids Dental Program if you don't have a dental plan and if you receive assistance with your Medical Services Plan premiums. Call your local health unit or family dentist for more information. It is recommended that you get dental information and advice by the time your child is age one. See page 64 for information on preparing your child for a visit to the doctor or dentist.

Looking After Your Child's Vision

Many people don't realize that vision is learned in early childhood, and that any problems in the clearness of vision for either eye can lead to perma-

nent vision loss if it's not treated early. At about eight to 12 months of age your child will start to develop hand-eye coordination and will be able to tell how close or far away things are. At about this time your toddler may be crawling and exploring freely, reaching for and touching things, and playing games like "peek-a-boo" and "patty cake." These are all signs that vision is developing normally.

If your child doesn't do these kinds of things, it may be a sign that you need to have her vision checked. Other signs that could mean vision problems include:

- Constant eye rubbing, squinting, or frowning.
- Blinking more than usual.
- Difficulty following an object with her eyes.
- Tilting or turning her head to use one eye only.
- Complaining that her head hurts.
- Both eyes not looking in the same direction (you may see this in a photograph).

Vision tests for toddlers do not involve alphabet letters and therefore a child does not need to be able to read. The eye doctor may use a special chart with pictures to test vision. Eye tests can even be done on children who are not yet talking. You can reassure your child that these tests do not hurt.

If you think your child has a vision problem, consult your doctor or eye doctor (optometrist or ophthalmologist). Some communities offer the Vision First Check Program–one free vision check for a child over two years old and under four years old. The program is a partnership with the BC Association of Optometrists. Call your local health unit for more information.

did you know?

If there is a vision or eye problem in your family, you should have your child's eyes examined by your eye doctor by the time she is age three.

Injury prevention is also important to healthy vision. **You can prevent eye injuries by:**

- Not allowing your toddler to play with darts, scissors, or missile-like throwing toys. Also be sure to keep toddlers away from older children who are playing with sharp objects.

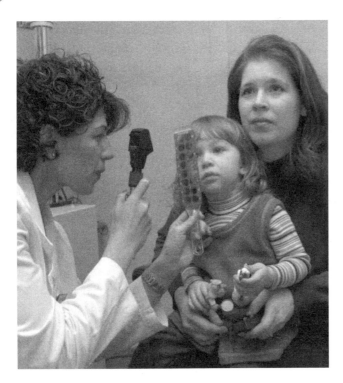

- Teaching children not to walk or run while carrying sharp objects like pencils, Popsicle sticks, or scissors.
- Keeping your toddler safely out of the way when you use power tools, lawn mowers, or chemicals and storing these tools in a safely locked place, because a toddler may try to use them when you are not watching.

Looking After Your Child's Hearing

Hearing plays a key role in how your child learns speech and basic language skills and is also important for social and emotional growth. Without good hearing, many learning experiences may be missed or overlooked, and learning how to speak will be much more difficult. Young children can't tell us about a hearing loss. Parents or caregivers need to notice when a child seems to be slow or behind in their development or when there are changes in behaviour such as not responding to new sounds or showing increased frustration.

Parents are excellent judges of whether their child can hear well. Check by asking yourself:

By six months, does your child sometimes:
- Turn her head in the direction of new sounds?
- Babble a lot of different sounds?
- Respond to her name?
- Respond to changes in your tone of voice?

By one year, does your child sometimes:
- Understand simple requests? *"Look here. Open your mouth."*
- Try to say words?
- Imitate different speech sounds?
- Like to repeat the sounds you make?
- Recognize words for everyday people and items? *"Where's Daddy?"*

By two years, does your child sometimes:
- Point to pictures when they're named?
- Listen to stories, songs, and rhymes?
- Use several different words? *"Mama, Dada, bottle, cat, ball."*
- Point to body parts when asked? *"Where's your nose?"*
- Follow simple directions? *"Get the ball."*
- Put two words together? *"My teddy."*

If your child is not doing these things at about these ages, talk to your public health nurse or public health audiologist (hearing specialist), or doctor. A hearing test should be considered in children whose relatives have had hearing losses early in their lives.

A Few Other Ear and Hearing Tips
- Don't smoke around your child or allow anyone else to. Second-hand smoke increases the risk of ear infections.
- When cleaning ears, don't use cotton swabs or anything in the ear canal.
- If your child is around loud sounds, such as music or fireworks, have her wear protection. If you wear ear protection as well, both your hearing and your child's will be protected.

did you know?

If you suspect a problem, *don't delay*. Even babies and toddlers can be given a hearing test. Early detection and treatment improves growth and development opportunities.

Protect Your Child with Immunizations

Immunizations are shots that help your child stay healthy. They work by preparing the body to fight certain diseases. Immunizations have dramatically reduced, or in some cases eliminated, diseases that caused severe childhood illness, and at times death. Although many diseases are no longer common, this doesn't mean they have disappeared.

By the time your child is six months old she has probably just had, or is due for, her third immunization. The first three shots begin to protect her health, but remember that booster shots are important to ensure that she gets full protection from disease. Boosters are given at 18 months.

If you have questions or concerns about immunizations, your public health nurse or doctor will have the most up-to-date and reliable information for you. For more information you can find the Canadian Paediatric Society's *Your Child's Best Shot: A Parent's Guide to Vaccinations* at your public library or local health unit.

As your child receives her shots, they will be recorded in her Child Health Passport and will follow the table below.

Your child will normally receive two shots (one in each leg) on each of the first three visits, one shot in her arm on the fourth visit, and two shots, usually in her arms, on the fifth visit at about one and a half years of age. After the shots you will be asked to stay in the office for about 15 minutes, so plan to have some toys or books with you for your child.

Reactions to Vaccines

- Most reactions are mild and do not last very long. The most common reactions are redness and swelling around the immunization site, a mild fever, crankiness, drowsiness, or loss of appetite. These may last for up to two days.
- If your child has a fever, bathe him in lukewarm water and give him extra fluids to drink. You can give him a child-sized amount of acetaminophen (a fever-reducing medication) to make him more comfortable. Do not give Aspirin to children.
- Reaction to the MMR (measles, mumps, and rubella) vaccine usually occurs within one to two weeks after the shot, and may include rash, slight fever, or swelling of the neck glands.
- If you're concerned about a reaction, talk to your public health nurse or doctor.

▶ **Q: "Should I delay a vaccination if my child is sick?"**

▶ **A:** Illnesses such as colds, coughs, or a low fever are not a reason to wait. Children with these illnesses respond normally to immunization. More serious illness on the day of the immunization may mean you should wait. Ask your public health nurse or doctor if you think your child may be too ill.

Recommended Basic Immunization Schedule

	1ST VISIT (2 months of age)	2ND VISIT (2 months after 1st visit)	3RD VISIT (2 months after 2nd visit)	4TH VISIT (12 months of age)	5TH VISIT (12 months after 3rd visit)	4–6 YEARS OF AGE
Diphtheria	•	•	•		•	•
Pertussis	•	•	•		•	•
Tetanus	•	•	•		•	•
Polio	•	•	•		•	•
Haemophilus Influenzae type b (Hib)	•	•	•		•	
Pneumococcal	•	•	•		•	
Meningococcal C				•		
Hepatitis B	•	•	•			
Measles				•	•	
Mumps				•	•	
Rubella				•	•	

► **Q: "I've heard about other immunizations like chickenpox, meningococcal, and pneumococcal vaccines."**

► **A:** A vaccine for children over one year of age has been developed that provides immunization for the chickenpox or varicella zoster virus. Meningococcal and pneumococcal vaccines are available for children over two months of age. These vaccines are not part of the basic immunization schedule that is paid for by the Ministry of Health. If you have questions about these vaccines, talk to your public health nurse or doctor.

When Your Child Is Sick

Children can go from being healthy to being ill surprisingly quickly. They may be playing happily one minute and then, unexpectedly, start feeling sick.

As a parent, you may have already learned the early signs of illness in your child. You might notice her eyes look glassy, she's crying a lot or clinging, or she may become very pale. Watching her and being aware of changes in her behaviour, play, eating, and skin colour can alert you to the early signs of an illness.

One mother says about her one-year-old daughter, *"I can always tell when she's coming down with something. She clings more and cries a lot—for no apparent reason. She just won't settle when I try to put her down for a nap."*

did you know?

• **Most healthy children have between six and nine viral infections every year. Some of these may be very short and mild. Others may last a week or longer.**
• **Your child's immune system actually gets stronger each time she gets a cold. So even the sniffles have their positive side!**

Colds

Colds are very common in babies and toddlers. Children who attend daycare or playschool may have more infections than children who are at home, since they are in larger groups. By the time your child turns three, you'll probably have plenty of experience dealing with a coughing, drippy-nosed toddler who feels grumpy and miserable and you will know how to keep your child comfortable.

did you know?

Colds are caused by viruses, and so cannot be treated with antibiotics. (Antibiotics only fight bacteria.)

Acetaminophen can lower your child's fever and may help relieve aches and pains. Two things that will help with a cold are getting lots of rest and drinking extra fluids. When your child is unwell, try to give him quiet time at home as much as possible. This will help him be more comfortable and will also reduce the number of people he can give his bugs to. Stories, videos, and extra cuddles will help your toddler cope with the discomfort of being ill.

A cool-mist vaporizer may help clear your child's nasal passages. For the sensitive skin around his nose, you can use a small amount of Vasoline to help protect the skin.

Consult your doctor if your child has a cold plus any of the following:
- earache
- fever lasting several days or higher than 38.4°C (101°F)
- sore throat and swollen, sore glands in the neck
- shaking, chills, and excessive sleepiness
- coughing that produces green or grey mucous or lasts more than 10 days
- chest pain or shortness of breath
- blue lips, skin, or fingernails

My Child Has a Fever

A normal temperature ranges from 36.4° to 37.4°C (97.6° to 99.4°F), with the average being 37°C (98.6°F). Many things can cause an increased temperature, including overheating when overdressed, being in a hot car, having a bath that is very warm, hard crying, active exercise in warm weather, or not enough to drink (therefore not enough fluid in the body—dehydration). These situations are easily corrected by providing a cooler environment and fluids.

Fever related to illness is a sign that the body is fighting a virus or bacteria. Although the fever itself is usually not harmful, it can cause dehydration and discomfort.

If your child has a higher-than-normal temperature, dress him lightly, offer plenty of fluids, and provide comfort. If his temperature is higher than 38.3°C (101°F), give him an age- or weight-appropriate dose of acetaminophen or ibuprofen (do not give Aspirin; see note below) and cool him down with a sponge bath in lukewarm water. See your doctor if you are concerned about dehydration.

Consult a doctor immediately if your child has a temperature of 39.4°C (103°F) or higher and has not been helped by the acetaminophen or ibuprofen and sponge bath—or if your child has a lower temperature and:
- Has a seizure.
- Is crying inconsolably.
- Has a rash.
- Has a stiff neck.
- Has difficulty breathing.
- Is confused or delirious.
- Has difficulty waking up.

did you know?

Acetylsalicylic acid (ASA) products (Aspirin, 222s, and 292s) are NOT recommended for children under 18 years because of the possibility of developing Reye's Syndrome, a serious disease of the liver.

Taking Your Child's Temperature

Simply touching your child's forehead or neck may tell you that she has a fever. To confirm this, you must take her temperature. If your child is crying, vomiting, cranky, has diarrhea, or is listless, drowsy, and hot, you don't need to take her temperature to know that she is not well. But you should take her temperature to know how high her fever is and how long she has had it. If you are calling your doctor, this is information that you will need to pass on to him or her.

The underarm method is recommended for children under six years of age, because if you use a glass thermometer in your child's mouth, there is a risk

that she will bite down and break it. You can take her underarm temperature using either a glass or a digital thermometer. Choose the one that is the easiest for you to read.

How to Take an Underarm Temperature
- If you're using a glass thermometer, wash it in cool, soapy water or rubbing alcohol to get it clean. Shake it down to below 36°C (96°F). If you're using a digital thermometer, press the button to turn it on and follow the manufacturer's instructions.
- Place the bulb of the thermometer high up in your child's armpit, making sure it's touching bare skin on all sides. Hold her arm close to her body, and wait at least five minutes for a glass thermometer and three minutes for a digital one. Plan to distract your child with something interesting—a video, story, or drink—in order to keep her still for the required time.
- If you add one degree to the reading, this will give you a reasonably accurate temperature of the body inside.
- Tell your doctor that this is an underarm temperature when you are giving this information.

What About Ear Thermometers?

Many doctors feel that ear (tympanic) thermometers should be used only with older children. Others say that these thermometers aren't always accurate. At the same time, some doctors do recommend ear thermometers for children as young as three months. These thermometers are more expensive than other types. **If you're interested in using an ear thermometer, talk to your doctor or public health nurse.**

did you know?

 Rectal thermometers are NOT recommended for home use.

A Visit to the Doctor

A visit to the doctor, either with a problem or just for a check-up, can be a stressful experience for your toddler. He's at a developmental stage when his fear of strangers is heightened, and this is a stranger who may need to touch him. How you prepare your child, your feelings about the visit, and his interaction with the doctor can make a lasting impression on his attitude toward doctors in the future.

When you know about a planned visit to the doctor, there are steps you can take to prepare your child to make it a good learning experience:

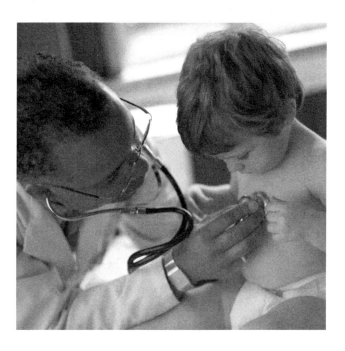

- Let him know where he's going, when, and why. Don't give too much information, but prepare him for what to expect. An older toddler will usually ask you further questions, e.g., *"The doctor will look in your throat and ears and you can sit on my lap the whole time."* Or *"The doctor is going to give you a shot in the arm. It will sting for a minute, but I'll hold you on my lap the whole time and we'll have a special treat afterwards."*
- Book the appointment for a time when your child is well rested and not hungry.
- Tell and show him what the doctor will do: look in his ears, in his throat, listen to his chest, and possibly weigh and measure him. Let him know that the doctor is there to help if he's ill.
- Have him play "doctor" to his teddy, and encourage him to use play about everything the doctor will do both before and after the visit.
- Bring along anything that will make your child more comfortable: a favourite blanket, teddy, or soother.
- You can find excellent children's books about visits to the doctor in your local library. Read these often with your child and answer his questions.
- After the doctor's visit, praise your child for his behaviour and efforts to cooperate (even if he cried the whole time). *"You held so still when the doctor looked in your ears!"*

Prepare your child, and prepare yourself for the visit. Think about your questions and write them down. Ask questions and express your concerns. Discuss anything that may seem out of the ordinary about your child's health. Take all the information you think you might need with you such as details about eating or bowel habits, his temperature, what has happened, and his immunization record.

If Your Child Has to Go to the Hospital

Sometimes we have warning that our children need to go to the hospital. At other times it's unexpected. When you know about a hospital visit, preparing your toddler and yourself will help to make it a comfortable learning experience.

Before thinking about how to get your toddler ready, prepare yourself. Make sure that you understand why your child is going and what she is having

done. Will she have a needle put into a vein and fluid through a tube (intravenous)? Will she have medication through a mask that puts her to sleep (anaesthetic) or medication to help her relax (sedative)? How long will she be in the hospital, and where and when can you be with her? This is some of the information you will want to know in order to prepare your child and yourself. Your child needs you to be with her as much as possible while she's in hospital. If it's impossible for you to be there most of the time, plan for relatives or close friends to fill in. Arrange for child care if you have other children at home, and take leave from your work if possible. If you have to decide between being with well children at home or your toddler in hospital, choose in favour of your toddler.

Toddlers can be very aware of their parents' emotions. If you are anxious or fearful, talk about these feelings to your child in a positive way. Say, *"I know I'll feel better when you're home again"* or *"Daddy will be right there when you wake up."*

As with any change in your toddler's life, don't think that surprising her will make it less stressful. Tell her where she's going and why in a way that she can understand. *"We're going to the hospital, where the doctor will put a tiny tube in your ears so that they won't hurt any more"* or *"We are going to visit the doctor and nurses at the hospital so they can fix up your eyes so you can see better."* See page 84 for information on helping your child deal with change in the family—many of these tips are also helpful when preparing for a visit to the hospital. Reading books, talking about the visit, and playing "hospital" with her dolls or teddy will help her understand exactly what will be

happening. If possible, go on a tour of the hospital so that your child becomes familiar with the people, sounds, smells, and sights there. Hospitals often have information booklets that may help you to explain to your child about the hospital visit.

Toddlers may be most worried about being "left" in the hospital away from their parents and family. In talking with your child, make sure she understands that you will be with her and that she'll be coming home with you after the procedure or stay is over. When you leave your toddler in the hospital, make sure she knows when you will return and that the nurses and doctors are there to help her. Taking some of her favourite things from home to the hospital (a favourite teddy or blanket, pyjamas, and some books) may comfort her. (Be sure to find out what you can bring into hospital, and to put your name on the things from home so that they don't get lost.)

Even the most well-prepared child is likely to have some reaction to the unfamiliar surrounding of a hospital. Don't be surprised if your child goes back to earlier comforts such as thumb sucking, clinging, and wanting a soother or bottle. Toilet training may also change, slow down, or need to be put on hold. These behaviours usually decrease and then stop soon after returning home.

Before you leave the hospital, make sure that you ask for and understand any instructions about your child's condition. Ask how much activity is allowed, what she can eat, what you should be looking for, and when you should be taking her to see the doctor again. If you are given medications for your child, be sure you understand how much, how often, and how you should give it to her (e.g., mouth or inhaled). Learn about any side effects, and what you should do if the medication is spit up.

Second-Hand Smoke

Second-hand smoke is a combination of the smoke from a burning cigarette, cigar, or pipe and the smoke exhaled by the smoker. This smoke contains thousands of different harmful chemicals, some of which cause cancer. **Remember that the smoke from one cigarette can stay in a room for hours, even if the window is open.** Another important point: you are setting an example for your child's future behaviour. Children of smokers are more likely to become smokers themselves and to suffer the health risks involved. So, protect your child by not smoking in your home or in his presence, and by making your car a smoke-free environment.

did you know?

Children exposed to second-hand smoke have higher rates of Sudden Infant Death Syndrome (SIDS), asthma, pneumonia, bronchitis, colds, ear infections, and sore throats because:
• **Their lungs are just developing and are easily damaged.**
• **They breathe faster than adults do, so they may inhale more pollutants.**

How Clean Does Your House Have to Be?

▶ **Q: "My friend Donna has the cleanest house and child I have ever seen! And then there's my daughter, covered with dirt two minutes after I wash her, and the floor covered with cereal. What's right?"**
▶ **Q: "Should I rinse, boil, or just blow on the soother when it's dropped?"**
▶ **A:** These are common questions. How clean is clean enough? With an active toddler at home you won't always have time to spend on cleaning. Here are some cleaning tips to help you make it through the day, but most importantly, to ensure that you get that quality time with your toddler:
• Try keeping all your cleaning supplies in an area of your home where they're easily ready for use. (NOTE: For safety purposes, keep cleaning materials locked out of your child's reach.)
• Clean when your toddler is napping.
• Plan how many areas of the house can be clean and need to be clear at one time. This may depend on how many naps your child has per day and where the main child play areas are in your house.
• Cleaning with soap and water will be fine; there is no need to use antibacterial soaps.

• Use a cleaning cloth/sponge. If you are reusing the same cloth throughout the day, wash your cloths/sponges frequently with your laundry and dry them in the dryer to freshen them up and reduce the bacteria on them.
• Disposable wipes are also quick and easy, and decrease the germ risk to your toddler.
• Never use the cloth that you use to wash other surfaces to wipe your toddler's face. This will help reduce the spread of germs and reduce infections.
• Encourage your toddler to help out with small chores as he grows, e.g., putting his blocks in a basket, helping with sweeping or vacuuming. This is a great life-learning experience for him. It promotes independence and self-confidence, and helps him feel like he's a part of the family.

Most of the really harmful germs that cause illness are spread from people or animals, not from dirt. So focus your efforts on cleaning up the things that are true germ-breeding spots, such as animal droppings, raw meat, used tissues, or open garbage bins. Also make sure that objects that are choking size (such as nuts, beads, or pins) are swept up from the floor.

Remember that an important factor in good hygiene is hand washing. Toddlers often eat with their hands and suck on their fingers, so focus your efforts on developing good hand-washing routines after using the toilet, before eating, and when your child is really dirty. Disposable wipes are useful for hand washing if you are away from home or a sink.

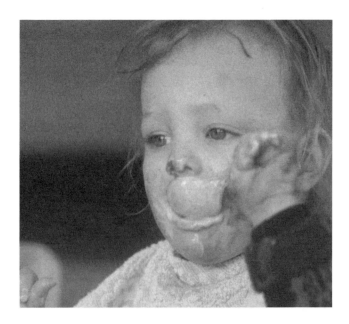

Parenting

••

Living with a Toddler

The days of putting your child down for a nap and returning to find her in the same spot after her nap are nearing an end. You may be getting more sleep, but you'll need the rest because your daily activities will be increasing very quickly. Food may begin flying, *"NO!"* may be a word ringing in your ears daily, and an ever-moving child may be delightful and very tiring all at the same time. As your toddler grows, both of you will be learning more than you ever thought possible. It may even make you long for the good old days when you sat up peacefully in the middle of the night for a cuddle and a feed.

This stage of development will keep you moving, and the rewards you experience will increase with each new skill. Your child will start understanding humour, play with you, smile back, and stroke your face lovingly. As some parents say, *"This is when the good stuff starts!"*

Remember that no parent does everything right all the time. Everyone makes mistakes. Look at these mistakes as a way to learn about yourself, about your child, and about your relationship.

Key Points to Remember
- Make sure you are providing a **safe place to grow** by childproofing your home.
- Be as **loving** and caring as possible.
- Relax, choose to support both yourself and your toddler by carefully thinking about what is really important and what is really only a small problem.

Life has changed forever. You will most likely never have as clean a house with a toddler as you did before children. Set new priorities: decide what needs to be done and what would be nice to have done. Let go of the unimportant things as you make sure you have time to play.

Try to use long-term thinking in any struggles you may have with your child. Ask yourself how important the issue is to her development or safety. Will it make a difference tomorrow or a week from now? The changes between six months old and three years old are big ones and you will need to plan different ways of working with your child as she grows older. You may find that going outside without a hat on isn't a big issue and not worth fighting about if the weather is not very cold and you are not going to be out a long time. You can suggest that she wear a hat rather than demand it, which takes the pressure off both you and your child. *"It looks cold today. This hat will keep your ears warm if you want it."* Keep the hat handy, of course, since your child may discover that you were right and want it two minutes later. If you keep a few important points such as safety in your mind all the time, your child will learn that when you insist on something it must be important. This is much better than your child being so used to arguing that it becomes a habit and she begins to tune you out. If the issue is important, let her know it. *"No, you can't play with the matches—you could be burned. I'll give you this toy instead."*

Learn to Compromise

Being the parent does not make you always right, nor does it give you the right to always make the decisions. Think of how you would feel if you always had to do what someone else told you with no chance to express what you wanted or liked. It is your job as a parent to guide your child, keep her safe, and help her develop the skills to be responsible.

If your three-year-old wants to be naked and you want her dressed for dinner, be creative. *"Which would you like to wear, your red or blue bathing suit at the table today?"* Or try using humour to change a situation, since an older toddler can see the funny side of things. *"You better put on your shoes or else the cat might wear them, and what would that look like?"*

Although children like to feel that overall you are in control, they are at a stage of development when they need to try it out for themselves. They are not testing *you*—they are testing their developing ideas or boundaries and powers. So give them choices, even if it is something they must do. *"Do you want to put on your coat first or your boots first?"* works much better than *"Put on your coat now."*

Whenever possible, avoid fights rather than trying to cope with them. Make sure your child is well rested and fed at regular times. Children like routines, and will be more co-operative if they know a certain thing happens at a certain time most days. A hungry, tired, cranky child is difficult for even the most experienced parent to deal with. If you know that you may be facing some difficulty, try to work around it with planning or moving to a different activity through creative change. For example, when leaving the park, first give your child warning that you'll have to leave soon. And when the time comes, say *"Let's go get in the car where you can listen to your Barney tape."* Or *"Do you think I can run faster than you to the house? Let's race."* When turning off the TV or video, teach your child which buttons to push so that the actual turning off becomes a fun and independent thing to do. (Of course, she will soon learn how to turn it on as well, which may present its own problems.)

> When your child shows you her new skill of putting playdough into the keyholes, take a deep breath, count to 10, and say to yourself *"I will be a coach, not a critic … positive not angry."*
>
> You could say something like *"You sure did a good job of putting all that playdough into such small holes, but please don't do it again because I can't get it out easily. Let's put some playdough into these little pots instead."*

Staying Cool As a Parent

What do you do when you've had it—your child has pushed your buttons one too many times today and you are tempted to start yelling and throwing food back at him? Step back, leave the situation, and calm down.

Take a deep breath and try to:
- Take a break. Put your child in a safe place like a crib, generally let your feelings out in a way that works for you. You can do this without involving your toddler in your own tantrum, which he would find frightening. As parents it is important to learn about ourselves so we can do this safely.
- Call your partner or a close friend and talk about the challenges of your day, preferably not in front of your toddler.

- Take a nap when your child does instead of cleaning up the house or doing other chores. You need rest in order to make good decisions.
- Find ways to reduce your own stress. Make time to practise yoga, take a walk, or play music. Make sure that someone you trust is looking after your child so that you can do these things without worrying.
- Get to know other parents and plan to share child minding so you know that you can get a break if you need one.
- Keep a diary of your day and note when and why you tend to blow up. If you notice a pattern, try to change the triggers of your temper. If you find that you are getting angry at dinner time when you are busy and your child is hungry, plan a late snack to keep him happy, or have a short rest together, or make some quiet time with a toy.

If you are feeling overwhelmed and afraid you might lose control and hurt your child, get help immediately. Put your child somewhere safe and call a friend, family member, or crisis line.

Prolonged or Intense Periods of Stress

Sometimes your life may seem particularly stressful beyond the normal demands of parenting. You may have too much to do, too little money, and not enough support.

If you know that this is happening to you, look for ways to reduce stress in your everyday life. Make a list of what has to be done, what needs to be done, and what would be nice to have done. Make sure you have time for yourself every day, even if it's 20 minutes in the morning before everyone is up, to think, stretch, do deep breathing, or have a bath. Although it may not be the first thought in your mind, reach out to others to help you. If you can, hire a housecleaner (even for two hours a week), organize a babysitter, or trade child care with another parent. Take care of yourself by eating well, exercising, and getting enough sleep. You are much more useful when you are feeling

well instead of being without sleep, hungry, or very, very tired.

As one mother said, *"When my father got sick and I knew that I'd be looking after him as well as my baby and my two-year-old, I made a list of all the things that I could let go of. I decided not to worry how clean the house was and I stopped baking muffins and bought them instead. I let the garden go and asked my husband to do the laundry. I knew I could go back to doing those things when I wasn't so stressed."*

Postpartum Depression

Postpartum depression is not the "blues," a "phase," or a small problem that will fix itself. One in five women with a new baby will experience postpartum depression. This will often happen within a year of their child's birth, although it may come about even later. **Without treatment** postpartum depression can stop a woman's ability to do daily tasks, to work, and to care for her children well.

What Does Postpartum Depression Feel Like?

You may:
- Feel irritable and frustrated with your child, partner, or family. You may be fighting and very angry about small problems. *"I was so tired I would yell about dirty diapers. How could I tell anyone I was so angry at this beautiful little baby?"*

- Not feel anything. You may have lost your sense of humour, not feel love or closeness with your child or partner, or generally feel numb or empty. *"Nothing seemed to be fun any more. I didn't even like my other kids. They just seemed to be in the way."*

- Feel unable to cope with any amount of responsibility or work. You may feel that what you do is pointless and that others could do it better than you do. *"I would lie in bed and tell myself to get up and clean the house or play with the baby, but then I would think, Why bother? It won't make any difference to anyone."*

- Feel overwhelmed with emotions and cry often, even at small things. *"Even the long-distance telephone ads made me sob, I felt so out of control."*

- Have panic or anxiety attacks, where you may have a racing or pounding heart, shortness of breath, shaking, sweating or chills, a choking feeling, intense fear you are dying, or a feeling that you are going crazy. *"It hit me so hard in the grocery store I thought I was dying. I ended up gasping on the floor with everyone looking at me."*

- Feel anxious and worried about your child, yourself, your family, or any number of other things. *"I would get up at night to check that our child was still breathing, and then have to check out the whole house that it was locked and safe."*

- Have thoughts of hurting your child, or yourself. *"I kept having this sudden vision of my child being killed in a car crash. I loved him so much, yet this kept coming at me. I felt like I would cause something to happen just by having these intense thoughts."*

You may also sleep too much or have trouble sleeping, be over- or undereating, feel unattractive, alone, and ashamed.

If you think you may have postpartum depression, get help. You cannot deal with this on your own. There is help that will make a difference and you need to talk to your doctor, public health nurse, or community agency so that you can get the help you need. Keep asking for help until you get it. You and your family need and have the right to an understanding helper.

You may be advised by your doctor to take antidepressant and/or anti-anxiety medications for a period of time. This usually helps you to feel better while the other changes and support you need are organized. A few other things you can do in your life to help you feel better are:

- Find a support system of people who can understand how you are feeling. One friend or partner may not be able to provide all the support you need. Try looking for postpartum depression support groups, counsellors, family members, public health nurses, or a few friends.

- Find some time for yourself every day when you stop being a mother. Get the help of your partner, family, or a babysitter so that you can get out on your own or with friends. If money is a problem or you are a single mother, consider trading child minding with another parent in a similar situation. Be careful, though, not to take on another child until you are ready to handle this. Perhaps you can "bank" some time that you will repay at a later date when you are well again.

- Be sure you get enough sleep, eat well, and get out for exercise regularly. It may be exhausting just thinking about physical activity, but try to start small—even if it's a walk in the park with your child—and work up to regular exercise.

- Talk about and safely act out your feelings, no matter how silly, sad, or angry the activity may seem to you (e.g., punching a pillow). Make sure that you and your child are safe when you do this. Have someone else look after your child, or do it when she's asleep, or just put her in her crib. Whatever time you choose, don't have your child part of this, since it will most likely frighten her. Let go, cry, pound a pillow, run around, scream in the car—find a way to feel your emotions.

The first step to helping yourself is talking to someone. If you think you have postpartum depression, contact your doctor, your public health nurse, or a postpartum support group today.

Resources

Postpartum Depression and Anxiety. A Self Help Guide for Mothers. To order, call 604-255-7999.

Postpartum Survival Guide by Ann Dunnewold and Diane G. Sanford.

This Isn't What I Expected: Overcoming Postpartum Depression by K. Kleiman and Valerie D. Raskin.

Internet site: postpartum.org

Discipline: Fair, Reasonable, and Consistent

The goals of using discipline are to teach and guide children to be safe, responsible humans with a healthy conscience, good values, and acceptable behaviour. Discipline should not be used to punish or to make a child obey, but rather to help him understand how to fit into the world in a thoughtful, healthy, and productive way.

Discipline should be:
- Based on respect for your child and his feelings. Name calling, blaming or talking in a hurtful way is not effective discipline.

Discipline needs to be:
- Seen as fair by the child (although he may not feel this at the time).
- Right for the child's age and what your child can do.
- Consistent, understood, and delivered at the time of the problem behaviours.
- Explained to the child, so the discipline becomes a learning experience.
- Designed to build upon the trust and love between you and your child.

Before You Get to Discipline

Prevent problems
It is always best to prevent behaviour that you do not want rather than deal with it after the fact. To help your toddler do the right things, organize your day so there are regular rests and mealtimes. Talk to her about changes, and think about how she responds to changes when you are planning activities. Regularly giving her attention, even when you are busy, will help her to resist attention-getting activities such as yelling, damaging objects, or throwing things.

Show the behaviour that you would like your child to show
Children learn about working with others and about communication, behaviour, and relationships by watching the people around them. Be very aware that your child is learning from you as you deal with daily situations and people. If you swear, don't be surprised to hear it coming from your toddler. If you react in an angry way, your child will see this as normal and what she should do. If you are polite and respectful, on the other hand, your child will learn about courtesy and cooperation. If you are fair, your child will learn about, and act out, being fair.

Be clear about limits and rules
Having fair and consistent rules helps a child to understand limits and behave in a way that works well with you and with groups. Rules should be simple enough that your child can follow them. They should fit with the age of your child (see page 77). An 18-month-old who scribbles on the wall may have his crayons taken away; a three-year-old may help to wash the wall. Being clear means saying exactly what it is you want. *"Food is for eating, not throwing"* is much more meaningful than *"Stop that!"* or *"Cut it out!"* and reminds your toddler what you want rather than what you don't want.

Praise good behaviours
Children learn quickly. If good behaviour is rewarded with attention and praise, and problem behaviour is responded to with understandable consequences (see forms of discipline below), they will soon focus on activities that work for them.

Help Your Child Behave

- Let your child know that you accept why he might be doing something. *"You want to play with the truck that your big brother is using…"*
- Let your child know that other children have needs too. *"But he is playing with it now."*
- Offer a solution. *"When Andrew finishes playing, then it will be your turn. I'll let you know when Andrew is finished or he can let you know."*
- Let your child know what the limits are and what is expected or what you want. If possible, state limits positively. *"We have to wash our hands before we eat."*
- Offer explanations for limits. *"You need to wash your hands to get rid of the germs that might make you sick."*
- Help children see consequences. *"The cat bit you because you pulled his tail. That hurt him."*
- Redirect. Give your child something else to do. *"If you draw on the wall, it is too hard to clean. Here's a piece of paper we can hang on the wall. You can draw on that."*
- Offer choices. *"You can't pour the milk on the table. But you can pour it into the blue cup or into the red cup."*
- Help children express their feelings and their desires. *"Do you want to tell Jamie that you don't like what he is doing? Try saying, 'Jamie, I don't like it when you grab my doll.'"* Help them solve problems. *"Jamie, I know where we can find you a doll and then you and Ann can play together."*
- Be consistent. Children need to know that you always respond in the same way if there is a limit. *"I can't drive you to the park until you are buckled into your car seat."*
- Let your child know what is going to happen. Toddlers find it difficult to cope with change. Your toddler may move from one situation to another more easily if you let him know what's going to happen and when it will happen. *"We will be leaving Jesse's house in a few minutes."*
- Hold or carry your child if he does something dangerous like running into the street. *"I am going to hold you because it is much too dangerous to run into the street. Let me know when you are ready to walk, holding my hand."*

Challenging Behaviours

Children do not come into this world naturally aware of how to work well with other children or with adults. The toddler years are when your child begins to learn what she can and can't do and how she can talk, work with, and learn from others while learning about herself and who she is. This is the time for you to help her learn the basic skills needed for thinking, caring, and behaving responsibly in the future.

Toddlers misbehave for a number of reasons, and very few (some would say none) of these reasons have to do with wanting to make you angry with them. Young children still see themselves as the centre of the world, with everything and everybody existing for their use and satisfaction. If they want a toy they simply go and get it, even if someone else is still playing with it. They also have little to no impulse control, so when a feeling arises they simply go with the first idea that comes with it, at times hugging you and at times biting out of anger. Toddlers can easily become frustrated with a lack of control over their world, and they don't yet talk well enough for you and others to understand them easily. *"Mom doesn't seem to understand that I want to play longer at the park and me saying 'No' isn't convincing her. I'm going to scream and throw myself on the ground. It feels good and may get the message across."* Toddlers are also at the developmental stage of learning independence and autonomy. Independence can come with acting out as your child exerts her will on those around her. Pushing other children away from their toys, throwing things they don't want, or screaming *"No"* are all ways your toddler might use to try to gain control over her world.

Other reasons your child will misbehave may have nothing to do with her developmental stage. A tired, hungry child or too many activities too close together can result in acting out or problem behaviour when she may normally be quite calm. More help with learning about what works in groups, and being shown how to use energy instead of being out of control can help with acting out. Changes in your home or routine can be unsettling for a child, and you may find that acting out increases until she settles down to a change. Finally, attention seeking may be the cause of acting out. If your toddler isn't getting the attention she needs, she may try misbehaving simply to get any attention, good or bad.

Although it's natural for a toddler to have challenging behaviours, it is your job as a parent or caregiver to help her to learn and practise skills that work well and are positive.

Ways to Help with Challenging Behaviours

Set a good example. If your toddler watches you being reasonable and calm, he is learning to work with frustration and stress in a healthy way. If he can see you deal with distress or strong feelings by talking through them with someone or taking a walk, he is learning about behaviours that work. If you hit, spank, or push when you are angry, frustrated or impatient, your child will most likely try to copy you. Always be around and watch children when they are playing together. Not only will you be able to step in if needed, but you will be able to use misbehaviour as a way to teach on the spot. Accept and support your child's feelings, both positive and negative. If your child is angry about having to share some food, say *"I can see that you are angry. That's okay, but it's not okay to hit your brother."* (It is also helpful to change the activity or play location and move on.) Be clear and consistent with rules. Let your child know why a behaviour is unacceptable. You may also need to repeat the message a number of times, since a toddler's memory is short. Every time you get on the bus repeat, *"You cannot run when we're on the bus, you might be hurt."* Encourage your child to use words instead of acting out to get what she wants. Young toddlers who are not yet able to talk well may need you to help with the problem. *"Are you mad that Breanne took your toy? Let's give her this ball and ask for your toy back."*

Biting

At one time or another your toddler will most likely try out biting. He may bite because he's curious, excited, frustrated, or angry. He may have seen another child bite and may be trying out this behaviour. Biting can also be used if there is nothing else to do or if the toddler needs attention. Sometimes toddlers bite simply because they are teething and it feels good.

Try to prevent biting by watching your child when he is playing with others and by giving him things that he can chew on, like teething rings. If your child is bitten or you see another child bite, use this example to talk about how biting is wrong and hurts.

What to Do If Your Child Bites

- State the rules clearly and simply. *"I can't let you bite. It hurts too much."* If your child bites while breastfeeding, a loud *"Ouch, that hurts. Don't bite!"* and removing her immediately from the breast will usually work.
- Don't bite back, even though this may be your first thought. It will only frighten your child and will not stop him from biting. Remember that you are the example.
- Don't laugh or take it lightly. Biting is not cute behaviour. A nibble on your leg may not seem serious, but a deep bite on a playmate is. Laughing will only increase the biting.
- After your child bites and you have been clear that this is against the rules, think about why it is that he has bitten and then take steps to change the situation. Is he tired, bored, frustrated, or angry? The behaviour may continue for longer when it is hard to figure out the "why."

Tantrums

Unfortunately, tantrums are a very normal event for toddlers. Young children are in a stage of development when frustration is high and they react quickly.

They want to be in charge of their environment, but don't have the language skills to do it effectively. They also become tired, hungry, and anxious easily. Toddler outbursts are usually more related to how well they are feeling than to the event that seemed to start the tantrum. It really wasn't saying "*No*" to the candy that threw your child over the edge; it was the end of the day and he was hungry, tired, and needed to go to the bathroom that made him so frustrated.

How to Avoid or Cut Down on Tantrums

- Make sure your child has regular rest and snack times. If you find your toddler often has tantrums when hungry or thirsty, give her food before going out and bring a snack along with you.
- Find helpful ways for your toddler to express her frustration or other strong feelings. This could be by running around in the park, throwing a ball as hard as she can, or expressing it verbally with your help. *"Are you mad at Jamie? Let's ask him for your truck back."*
- Let your child know ahead of time what is going to happen and what you want her to do. Toddlers find it hard to change activities without warning.

- Make reasonable rules when necessary, and think twice before saying an automatic *No* to requests. See page 78 for tips on what's really important in relation to discipline.
- Give your child control over little things in her life. Let her choose which clothes to wear or which cup to drink from. This can help to fulfill her need for independence and decrease her frustration level.
- If you see that your child is heading into a tantrum, try moving her to something else or changing the scenery with a quick trip into the yard or a ride on a play toy. If you know that she's losing control because she is hungry or tired, give her some food or quiet time.

What to Do When Your Child Has a Tantrum

- If the tantrum is already underway, don't try to stop it or talk with your toddler. She is out of control and can't stop herself. She will not be able to hear much of what you say.
- Stay calm and near your child. Your toddler needs to know that you are cool and in control. Having your own tantrum will only frighten her as well.
- Some children are better able to move back into control if they are held firmly but lovingly, in a hug or cuddled on the floor. Others find this closeness even more frustrating and will become worse.
- Ensure that your child is somewhere safe, where her flailing, rolling, or pounding won't cause damage to herself, others, or property. If you are in a public place, you can sit beside her or go into a change room, go outside, or pick her up and take her to the car. Once you have her in a more private place, sit beside her and let the tantrum run its course. If your child is in a shopping cart, you can put your arms around her to make sure she doesn't fall out, and simply keep her in the cart until the tantrum is over.
- If you are in a public place, try to tune out the audience your child will most likely have attracted. If you appear calm and in control of the situation most people will understand and give you the space you need. Many people have been in the situation themselves. If, on the other hand, your anger is getting the best of you, some may want to step in and help you.

- When the tantrum is over, cuddle and comfort your child and tell her that you are happy she's feeling better. Praise her for moving back into control. Don't punish or go into any lengthy talk about the tantrum—she will have had enough. At this point it's time to learn about why the tantrum happened and work out a way to change the situation. Is your child tired, hungry, or frustrated?
- Don't give in to whatever the tantrum may have been about. You do not want your toddler to learn that a tantrum will change your mind.

Fighting

If you've had your child around other playmates or siblings, you will have already noticed that they don't always get along peacefully. Toddlers are beginning to understand ownership and want to exert control over those around them, playmates included. Since your child is likely to have at least a few fights in his toddler years, think ahead about how you will handle it when he fights.

One approach is to stay out of it and let the children come up with solutions on their own. It is thought that this method gives a child the opportunity to think through problems and helps them learn without someone else stepping in to help them. The younger the child, the more you will need to be a coach. If someone is being hurt or if the children are not on an equal footing—for example, if one is larger or older than the other—you will need to step in.

Another way to deal with fighting is to step in and help the children in a fair manner, offering your solution. This method has the advantage of emphasizing fairness and caring for each other rather than who was right, which may often be the toddlers' concern. *"Let's try to share the toy"* or *"Can you take turns?"* may be your view, whereas a toddler may see the situation as *"It's mine and I want it now."*

Although it may be disturbing to see your child or children fight, think and talk things through and try things that may help her learn a new skill. Talk about this with another adult who may be able to help you. Toddlers are still very self-centred and react quickly, so don't be too surprised if your little angel swings at her brother when he takes her toy. With your coaching, an older child may be able to learn what works

with a toddler and how to play with a toddler. Just make sure that safety and learning can both happen and that part of what is being learned is fairness.

Whining

▶ **Q: "Nothing sends me around the bend faster than hearing my three-year-old whine. What can I do to stop this behaviour?"**

▶ **A:** Whining, which is that unpleasant tone between talking and crying, can bring some of the most experienced parents to the end of their rope much more quickly than biting or other challenging behaviours. Whining is often a call for attention, or a result of boredom, hunger, fatigue, or illness. In order to prevent whining in your toddler:

- Watch how you communicate. Do you tend to whine yourself?
- Take note when there is no whining and comment on how pleasant it is to hear a normal voice.
- Avoid the common causes of annoying behaviour in toddlers, such as fatigue and hunger. See page 72 for more information on challenging behaviours.

The next time your toddler starts whining, try saying "I can't hear you when you talk like that. I'll listen when you talk in your real voice." Also, don't give in to the demands of the whining, or your toddler will soon learn that this is a way to get you to give in.

Dawdling

Dawdling probably has as much to do with our busy lives as it does with children's development. If we weren't in a hurry, we might not notice that our child is taking a long time to do things. Time does not have the same meaning for young children as it does for adults. We often view our day as being driven by time—we get up at seven, leave the house at eight, and start work at nine—but these numbers mean nothing to a toddler who is interest- or activity-focused. Getting up in the morning means they get to play again and see their family, and getting in the car means they are going somewhere.

Moving from the house to the bus may normally be a two-minute walk for you. With a toddler in hand this walk can extend into a 10-minute tug of war, with you encouraging *"Come on, let's go"* and your toddler looking at everything on the sidewalk that he already saw yesterday. This isn't to make your life difficult; it's normal curiosity and interest. A toddler's attention can quickly move from one activity to another. Although they may want to obey you and get moving, there are a dozen things, such as toys, noises, and people, which will be more interesting to them between their bed and the bathroom.

Knowing that dawdling is normal doesn't make it any easier for parents to deal with. It takes patience to stand and wait for your child to put on his shoes (*"I do it!"*) while the clock is ticking and you're late for an appointment. Since it's almost impossible to stop your child from dawdling, plan ahead so that his pace doesn't cause you stress and frustration.

Dawdling Tips

- Give your child plenty of warning about leaving one activity and starting another. Don't expect the child who is in the middle of playing to drop everything instantly in order to go with you to the grocery store. Give him time to finish off one thing before beginning another.
- When you are organizing your day and week, build in the dawdling time that your toddler may need. Leaving in the morning may take your child an hour, so set the clock a little earlier and take your time instead of rushing and starting the day with you both unhappy.
- Tell your toddler what you want clearly and simply. Saying *"Hurry up, we're late"* is fairly meaningless to a child. Saying *"What do you want to put on first, your coat or your shoes?"* helps him to break a large task into manageable, bite-size pieces and gets him moving at the same time.
- Take whatever it is that he's interested in along with you. *"What a pretty pine cone. Let's take it with us and look at it on the bus."*
- Get rid of extras when you are in a hurry. Turn off the TV, put toys away, to make moving forward easier.

Some children's challenging behaviours, such as huge tantrums and acting out, may be the result of a language delay, a physical problem, or a sensory problem, such as hearing loss or eye problems. If you are concerned about your child's behaviour, consult your doctor or public health nurse.

Age-Appropriate Discipline

Six Months to One Year

Children under one year of age are only beginning to develop a sense of themselves as being separate from others. They do not plan to misbehave, but are simply showing you their needs and fears in the only way they know how. A one-year-old who spills his milk is not trying to be bad, but may simply be trying to move the glass, maybe with some frustration. These skills all together DO take practice. At this age it's important to help your child control his behaviour. A regular schedule of rest, feeding, and play will help. A lot of activity at once may bring out behaviours that you may find a problem. Again, he is not misbehaving, but rather showing you his discomfort or unhappiness. It is helpful for your toddler to learn about frustration and how to comfort himself. This means that you don't always have to pick him up the moment he fusses, or help him as soon as he can't reach a toy. Encourage and provide hints that will help him to discover new ways of thinking about things and calming or soothing himself first. Time out, consequences, or spanking (see forms of discipline below) are not useful and can be damaging for this age group. Moving to a new activity, spending quiet time with you, or giving your child a comfort toy are better supports.

One Year to Two Years

It is normal for children in this age group to try out independence and to try their will against yours. They are not being difficult just "because." They are simply testing their control over the world around them. You may notice this testing with an activity like climbing to see just how far they can go, or in a completely different way such as continuing to do something that you have moved them away from. Try to be calm as they try out their new-found power—the desire to explore, along with a short memory span, makes safety a very important concern for this age group. Do not hesitate to stop your child with a firm *"No"* if she's doing something unsafe. Follow up the *"No"* in a simple way that she can understand, such as *"No, hot"* or *"No, dirty."* Remember that she can understand much more than she can say. Once you have stopped the unsafe behaviour, move her onto a safer activity.

Time out—removing the child from her surroundings—doesn't work well for this age group. It may be unsafe and can be scary because young toddlers are still establishing a sense of trust and have a fear of being left alone. They fear you won't come back. Being separated from their caregivers could create more fear than the hoped-for understanding of why the separation happened. Understanding challenging behaviours and simply moving to a new activity is the best way to guide your toddler's actions at this age. If your child is pulling glass bowls out of the cupboard, remove the bowls saying, *"Let's use the plastic ones."* Then redirect or move her onto the plastic containers (and, of course, move the glass ones up to where she can't reach them). Be sure to use your words for the activity, not the child. *"I can't let you hit your brother. Hitting hurts. You can hit the pegs on the pegboard, not your brother."* Taking a moment to think about what you are really upset about may help you in doing this.

Two Years to Three Years

Your child's frustration level will be high at this age as he begins to learn and understand what he's allowed or able to do. Temper tantrums or outbursts are an outlet for this frustration, and are not aimed at you. A toddler of this age will continue to try out behaviours. The best response is a caring approach that your toddler understands and you use in generally the same way each time. Be careful not to label your child as a *"Bad boy."* Talk about the behaviour or activity, not the child. For example, *"Throwing blocks is dangerous"* instead of *"You are a bad boy for throwing blocks."*

Discipline Methods

Time Out or Take a Break?

Time out continues to be talked about by expert early childhood teachers and caregivers; however, there is no clear decision on whether time out is useful or a problem. Many experts do not think that time out should be used with a young child under age three. Supporters of time out believe it allows your child to settle himself if he's upset and may also keep him from getting attention that increases the problem behaviour.

As mentioned, experts are concerned about how time out is used, especially with young children. Other names for time out are "a cool down," "take a break," "a time away," "a quiet time," or "sit and watch" as useful ways to work on or change behaviour. The reasons for time out and redirection are:

- To give everyone a chance to gain control in a safe place. When the child returns to the activity or goes back to the family or group, she can be successful.
- To teach children to know when their emotions are moving to a dangerous level and to know when they are ready to work with the family or in a group again.
- To allow the family or the rest of the group to continue their activities.

Most early childhood teachers and caregivers believe there are more effective ways to redirect toddlers and support their learning (see suggestions below). Educators strongly suggest that if time out is used, it must be used in a way that does not isolate the child, and is sensitive to the child's ability to understand why it is being used. (This is still being questioned with older preschoolers as well.) Time out should support further learning. All discipline must be calm and respectful, not angry or threatening.

- Give time outs only when your child understands that he's done something wrong, not for a first-time problem.
- Time passes slowly for toddlers. Time out should last no more than one minute for each year of your child's age, up to a maximum of five minutes, and should not be used for children younger than age three. Less time is better than more.
- Choose a place for time out that is safe and near you in the same room.
- Let time out be a quiet time to give your child the chance to calm down. Give your child something quiet to do such as a book to look at or a puzzle to do. After the time out is finished, praise him for sitting quietly and remind him what is it you want him to do. *It seems like you are ready now to play safely with the toys.*

Consequences

If your child pours her bubbles out on the grass knowing that it's wrong, don't leap up to get her some more. *"That's too bad—the bubbles are all gone now."* Children learn quickly that some actions have consequences: *"If I throw my blanket in the dirt, I lose it until it's cleaned."* Or *"If I refuse to wear a hat, my ears will get cold."* Using consequences as discipline can remove you from being the lawmaker all the time and still teach your child that her actions result in positive or negative outcomes. Consequences are generally best used with an older toddler because the ideas may not be easy for your child to understand. If you use this, be sure that your child's thinking is far enough along to understand consequences.

Redirection

Early Childhood Educators work with many different children with many different types of behaviour challenges. They have found that most toddlers respond well to caring, supportive, and repeated redirection that helps the child learn about "what to do" rather than "what not to do." The story is about redirecting the child, and finally moving the toddler from one activity into another.

G, age 3, is playing on the kitchen floor with plastic building blocks. His seven-month-old brother is playing beside him. Bored with building and looking for something different to do, G begins throwing the blocks as high as he can over the top of the baby's head. After several creative throws of the blocks and several requests from his mom to stop, G has not changed his actions. His mom is worried and frustrated that he is not doing as he is asked. What should she do?

When the behaviour first happens, she should go to the child. She should get down to his level to get his attention by gently touching his arm or his throwing hand and simply state again what she wants him to do, for example, *"G, throwing blocks in the kitchen is very dangerous. You might bump the baby or break something. Blocks are for building. Show Mummy what you can build with the blocks."*

Mom begins to stack the blocks, stays close but then steps back a little to see what G will do. G does not stack the blocks, but starts to throw them again, so Mom moves in closer and gently steers him toward the container of blocks and says, *"Throwing blocks is dangerous. Let's use them for building."* She then moves with the child to a different part of the kitchen, sitting with him to help him start using the blocks for building.

Using his natural curiosity and a little "scientist" thinking, Mom says, *"Let's build a tower together. I wonder if we can use all the blocks to build a really big tower!"*

Things are going along okay for a few moments. Mom praises him, *"Look at how tall your tower is and you are using the blocks so safely!"* The phone rings, taking Mom's attention for a moment, and the blocks are flying again.

Mom puts down the phone (best to call back later) and goes to G again, saying, *"G, I can see you are having some trouble using the blocks safely. I want you to put them away now and find something else to do."* She helps him put the blocks away. He may be upset. If so, she needs to let him know she is thinking about his feelings. *"You feel sad because you like playing with the blocks. When you are ready to use them safely, you can play with them again. Let's do that puzzle you like!"* Or she might give him a choice, *"What would you like to do, read a book or play with your dump truck puzzle?"* She needs to help him find a new toy and play quietly with him. She can compliment him, pointing out that he seems to be feeling better and that's great!

If instead of moving to the new activity easily, G resorts to temper, his mom will need to use the suggestions made in the "temper tantrum" section.

When this happens with your child, you will likely have to repeat the process many times before he really understands. Be positive, be caring. This type of discipline will help you to:

- Help your child to learn from you by seeing your self-control. He will understand that he has many choices.
- Increase your child's self esteem and self-confidence by showing him he can control himself and make good choices. It will show him that you care about him and are willing to support him.
- Reduce his confusion by making it clear what you want. He should also know what will happen if he runs into difficulty.
- Have a stronger, healthier, more trusting relationship with your child based on kindness, caring, and support rather than ending up in a power or control struggle.
- Support healthy development (including his brain power!) in all areas by providing a supportive and caring home for him.

> **Remember that nobody is perfect. Make sure that what you think your child should do is something that she can do at her age and ability. Know that you may be wrong at times as well. There are very few parents who don't yell at one time or another, or lose their temper. When this happens, follow up with your child, saying, "I'm sorry I yelled at you, but I was afraid that you would drop the vase." This not only lets her know that you are human just like her, but that mistakes can be dealt with and corrected. If you find yourself frustrated and yelling a lot, talk to someone who can help you change this.**

Say what you mean and mean what you say. Be clear about what you're asking of your toddler. Saying *"Cut it out"* or *"You're driving me crazy"* will not mean much to your child and won't help her stop what she's doing. *"Please put that down"* or *"Come here now, please"* are clear statements that your child can understand and do. Mean what you say: don't glance up from your paper and say, *"Stop it"* and then go back to your reading. If you are asking your child to do something (or to stop doing something), follow through and check that she's heard you and is changing her behaviour.

Spanking Is a Hot Issue

Disciplinary spanking is defined by the Canadian Paediatric Society as "physically non-injurious, is administered with an opened hand to the buttocks, and is intended to modify behaviour. Slapping the face, kicking, punching, arm-twisting, shaking, pinching, ear pulling, jabbing, shoving, choking, beating, or delivery of repeated demoralizing blows to a child, and spanking that produces bruising are not discipline, but rather is abuse."

There are different ideas in Canada in relation to spanking. More and more experts think that spanking is not a useful way to discipline a child. However, there are those who believe that spanking a child in a controlled manner, when other ways have not worked to get an important message across (such as safety) should be the right of a parent. There are others who believe that a child should never be spanked, no matter what the situation. This group believes that there are other, better ways to change a child's behaviour.

There is disagreement about the results of spanking, since there simply isn't enough scientific research to prove that controlled disciplinary spanking harms or works well. Some research shows that children who are spanked are more likely to be violent in their age groups and with their own children later in life. Others feel that you must look at all the child rearing to learn why some children learn to use force as a method of getting what they want.

When thinking about spanking as a form of discipline, think about what you want your children to learn from you. There are many other, more effective ways of teaching behaviour that do not use spanking

(see page 77 for tips on discipline). When your child is spanked, he is learning that physical force is how you work through problems. As well, he will not learn about other ways to work out a problem, such as talking through a problem (communication), re-directing, cool down, or quiet time. Spanking does not give your child the chance to learn from his actions, but will show him deep hurt and make him feel very unimportant, sad, and maybe hopeless. **Early Childhood Educators do not recommend spanking for any reason.**

It is important to remember that young children are small and cannot get help if they need it. They need to feel that adults can control themselves and will protect the child from harm. If you need help to control your anger, or if you would like to learn about different discipline ways, find a parent support group or parenting classes in your community. **Contact your public health nurse for information.** Help lines or crisis lines can provide on-the-spot advice for adults who are stressed or angry. Find out if there is a parent help line or crisis line in your community and post the number near your telephone so if you are too upset, you can quickly phone.

Being A Father

The To Do List: Life with a Toddler

Boy, do I feel dumb some days.
And tired.
And cranky.
And just hopelessly lost.
I've never been happier.

Emily was born a year ago this Sunday. She took her first steps yesterday.

In the past year, she has brought to our lives joy, fear, pain, delight, worry, arguments, laughs, back injuries, crib issues, self-doubt, and a clearer understanding of projectile vomiting than I think either of us ever wanted. But, really, it's the next bit that scares me.

There's a lot of talk about what to call the time between six months and three years. Some books call it one thing, others another.

I think it's the age when your baby becomes a person.

Let's face it. No matter how much you love your child and think she is clearly the most amazing baby anyone has ever had, for the first half-year babies spend the better part of the day sleeping, eating, and thinking up creative ways to get rid of that food. Around six months, all that begins to change.

Suddenly the squishy little thing in the blanket starts to laugh and burble. They begin to chat, and then walk (or walk, then chat—it doesn't matter which comes first really), then run, climb, jump, sing, shout, dance, and generally just grow up into a real human. The experts say that almost all the most important development happens in the first three years.

The scary part is, you're responsible for the whole thing. For making sure they are safe, happy, well fed, learning new stuff, growing strong: in short, for preparing their brains and bodies for the life ahead of them.

There are days when, like that guy in the car commercial, I wonder how I became completely responsible for another human being. What if I screw up?

Luckily, at least part of this process seems to happen without my assistance. When I come home from work I find myself stunned at the number of things my daughter seems to learn each day (and perhaps a little jealous of the people who got to watch her learn them).

Watching and copying my wife and me, Emily seems to have learned more about us and how we do things than we actually knew ourselves. A short list of the revelations includes:

- Sometimes we're not as gentle with the cats as we could be.
- It's acceptable, if everyone else is talking, to talk louder or even shout to make yourself heard.
- It's okay to hunt through the clean laundry basket and throw things you don't need on the floor (this one's my fault).

I don't think it's possible to think one's way through all the possible consequences of being the model for another human. Part of being a parent seems to be jumping in and accepting that your world will just be a bit different from here on in.

As I force myself to swear less, spend more time outside, and change the way I watch television, I can feel my day-to-day world slowly shift gears. I still seem to be the same person inside, but all the outside bits, many of the things I do in a day, look different. It's hard not to feel a touch sorry to lose some of that independence, but it doesn't seem a great cost for being someone's hero.

Unfortunately, part of being a hero means finding a way to tell your children *"No"* when you need to. When possible, avoid situations that you know will result in an argument by offering your child other choices. When you can't get out of a situation by distracting your child, be firm, make sure that any consequences are reasonable and fit the situation, talk to your partner to make sure you agree on the situation, never say anything you don't intend to carry out, and carry it out without anger.

From what I've seen, disciplining your child never gets easier. Nor should it.

Another change is the arguments. No matter how you slice it, my wife and I fight more these days. Of course it doesn't help that neither of us has had a really good sleep in a year or so, but I think the real shift is that we are constantly aware of being watched. The knowledge that your child is learning from the way you treat your partner, and how you let your partner treat you, seems to increase the amount of tension in the house. We find ourselves looking at all the things we do to each other and saying, "Am I being lazy, or inconsiderate here? Is there a better way?" It's exhausting.

So we stop and take stock. A lot. It's amazing what a babysitter and an afternoon picnic can do to make things look a bit better.

But the key to true happiness as a father is the games. I say, without shame, that I will do almost any stupid, goofy thing to hear my daughter laugh and there is nothing in the world like the expression of a child when you get down on the floor and start to play *their* games. I will wear whatever Emily gives me to put on, make that face *again*, read that book that I *can't stand* for the 30th time, just to see the delight in her eyes.

When I play with my child, I see the world through her eyes. All the things I had come to take for granted—my life, my wife (forgive me, dear), my day, that big blue coat in the closet—stand out now, shining and vibrant in the warmth of her smile.

So these, then, are my things to do today:
Love my family,
Keep them safe,
Teach my child to grow strong and happy,
Play,
And play,
And play.

I think that's about it.

Getting Active and Having Fun with Your Child

It isn't surprising that being overweight (obesity) has become a very real health concern for adults as well as children. Many of us spend too much time in front of the television and the computer, or sitting in the car. By getting active and up off the couch, gathering the family, and going out you can make a difference. Walk or bike whenever you can, park a few blocks from where you are going and walk the rest of the way, use the stairs, or simply play actively with your children.

Regular activity is good for all members of your family. You will find that you and your family have better health, weight control, more energy, improved fitness and self-esteem, stronger muscles and bones, better posture, and reduced stress. Activity combined with healthy food choices can help new mothers go back to their pre-pregnancy weight and size.

When you have a toddler, you may think you are active enough. To stay healthy or improve your health, you need 60 minutes of light effort each day. This can be in 10-minute "bites" of activities, such as easy walking or stretching. If you do moderate activities such as brisk walking, swimming, or cycling, you can cut it down to 30 minutes, four days a week. For further information, read *Canada's Physical Activity Guide*, which gives examples of activities that could work for you. Plan to build physical activity into your routines at home, at school, at work, at play, or on the way. The guide shows you how to make active living as natural as brushing your teeth or wearing a seat belt. Get a copy from your health unit or off the Web: www.hc-sc.gc.ca/hppb/paguide/intro.html.

Even though your toddler may not be "exercising," following you will be starting her on a habit that will last a lifetime. A family that is active together is helping themselves and setting an example for their children to follow. Spend time together and do fun activities such as running in the yard, going for a swim in the community pool, or walking on the beach or in the park. When your child is young you can put her in the stroller or back carrier and go for an active walk. You'll get exercise and she'll get fresh air and a chance to see new things and hear new sounds. When she's old enough, she'll want to do the

things that you enjoy, which may be going for walks with you. Exercise will be as natural and normal as having lunch.

If you are doing yoga or an exercise class, ask your teacher if your child can join in. You may find that your exercise time is more fun with a little "copy cat" beside you trying to follow along. If you are doing an upper-body workout, use your toddler as the weight. Of course you must be careful not to drop her, but you can do "presses" while holding her safely—she will love the attention and physical play and you'll get some exercise.

A word of caution about home exercise systems: toddlers can be easily injured on equipment such as treadmills, stationary bikes, or rowing machines, or by free weights. Make sure that you are with your child around these machines. When you are using this equipment, know where your child is and make sure that she's well out of the way. If you use a skipping rope to exercise, make sure it's stored away where your child can't get it, since a rope could wrap around her neck and cut off her breathing.

Many parks have play areas for toddlers, with slides, swings, and climbing equipment. Pools and recreation centres offer activities for parents and children to enjoy together as well. Getting together with other parents and their toddlers is good for all. In order for both you and your child to continue to enjoy the activities you do together, change them once in a while. You can try her favourite! For example, one day your toddler can choose to play with a ball in the backyard with you, and the next day she can go in the stroller for a walk. A variety of activities keeps everyone interested.

Parents Need Time Too

Even though you feel good about being a parent, spending all your time with infants and toddlers can be stressful and may not allow you to think about yourself at all. It's important that you regularly find time to stop being a parent and look after yourself without feeling guilty about having interests outside of your child! As well, your child will learn from seeing you take care of yourself, have interests and friends, and actively participate in your community.

Having time alone or with your partner often takes planning, from booking sitters or exchanging child care with a friend, to making meals for your child. It may seem as though getting out on your own is more effort than it's worth. Remember, you are most effective as a parent if you look after yourself, eat well, and get enough rest. Allow yourself some time away from your child to have adult fun. Even if your child objects, tell yourself that you will be a better parent when you return.

Many parents get support from talking to other parents. For this reason, many communities provide activities for parents to meet each other, to discuss the ups and downs of child rearing, and to share ideas. Parent discussion groups, parenting classes, and parent and tot drop-ins are three such community supports. Some organizations offer drop-in child-minding services, clothing exchanges, and toy libraries, as well as counselling programs. **For more information on parent supports, contact your public health nurse, your community centre or local family centre, or your local Y. Some churches, schools, and recreation centres also offer these services.**

Changes in Your Family

Toddlers are most comfortable with a regular daily plan so they can be uncomfortable with change in their lives. A regular plan means knowing what will happen and that knowledge gives young children a feeling of safety in spite of change in their lives. Some children react very strongly to changes in their lives while others don't seem to notice them. Babies and toddlers may not be able to talk about their feelings in words, so when there is a change in their lives, they may show you how they feel by:

- loss of appetite
- spells of crying
- nightmares
- outbursts of anger or temper tantrums
- clinging
- sleep problems
- being very quiet or withdrawn
- going back to old habits (thumb sucking, a bottle, wearing diapers)
- having trouble separating from parents or caregivers

Parents can help children who are going through changes by showing them that they are loved and that they will always be taken care of. When a change is coming, parents can think about their child's usual way of behaving to know what to expect. If a toddler has always had strong reactions and does not like to try new things, he may act out in his usual way. If a toddler is more comfortable with change, he may go through a big change with almost no change in behaviour.

If possible, let your toddler see that you can do things to help yourself deal with change. Young children can't be a support for you when things are difficult. Remember they are young, so find a friend who can help you. They need to know that you can look after yourself and them.

Sometimes change is welcome in our lives, and at other times it's hard. If you are unhappy with a move, stressed by a breakup or some other change, try to find a helpful person who can listen to your feelings and concerns. Let your child be a child, which means he should not need to help you with your safety or how you feel. If you are crying, tell your child that you are upset right now but will feel better soon, and that it's not his fault. If you need to, have a safe, caring person look after your child while you talk with a friend, talk with your doctor, or get help from a crisis centre.

You Can Prepare for Some Changes

There are some changes that you know about, such as the birth of a new baby or a move to a new house. Children can understand change if you tell them about it and talk with them. The older the child and the more important the change, the earlier you will want to get ready for the change. The following are

some ways of preparing your child for a change. (If your change is sudden, such as a separation or death in the family, you can still try some of these ideas. See page 91 for information on separation and page 92 on death.)

- Talk about the coming change in a positive way. *"Your new room will be a pretty blue colour"* or *"You will meet so many new friends at daycare."* If you are staying in a hotel or at a friend's house for a while, instead of saying *"It will be crowded, so you have to be good,"* try this approach: *"Let's pretend we are camping out, and good campers keep the campsite tidy."*

- Read books to your toddler about the changes you know are coming.

- Provide toys that allow your child to act out the change, such as a baby doll if a new baby is coming or a moving truck if you're going to a new house.

- Try not to have other changes at the same time, such as moving to a bed, starting toilet training, or changing from the bottle or soother.

- Your child's concerns are real for him, even if they seem silly to you. If keeping a favourite teddy or pair of shoes out of the moving box helps, then make sure they don't get packed away.

- Talk to your child about how things will be okay. Be warm, loving, and listen to your child when she shows you how she is feeling. Children need to know that their parents will take care of them no matter what else is going on in the world around them. Try to make time every day for the usual things your child enjoys, such as a favourite story, food he likes in his special bowl, or cuddle time before bed.

Welcoming a New Baby

▶ **Q: "Since bringing our new son home, the biggest baby in the house seems to be our three-year-old. She's wetting her pants after being toilet trained for six months, is cranky, whiny, and keeps asking for a bottle. We thought she was ready for being a big sister—what did we do wrong?"**

▶ **A:** How your child changes when a new baby is in the house will depend on a number of things, such as the age of your child (older is better), the way your toddler usually responds to changes, and

how much he knows and understands. It does help to know that it is very common for a toddler to be upset by the cute little baby who needs so much caring for. Young children don't like changes in their day or any change in the amount of time with their parents. A new baby in the house changes routines and takes time that would be the toddler's time.

Here are some ways to help with making the coming of a new baby easier for all of you.

Preparing for the New Baby

- A few months before the baby is due, let your child know that she will have a new brother or sister. Answer any questions she may have, such as where the baby will come from, in a way she can understand. Let your child feel the baby kicking and help her to talk to the baby "in your uterus."

- Read books about babies and big brothers or sisters. Look at your child's own baby pictures and talk about what she was like as a baby. If possible, visit friends who have infants and let her see what a baby looks, sounds, and smells like.

- If there will be changes in your home because of the baby, such as a new baby's room, moving out of the crib to a bed, toilet training, or even a change of houses, try to make the change before or after the baby comes so that these changes are not only because of the new baby.

- Find a baby doll for your child to "mother," just like Mommy and Daddy do. She can breastfeed, change a diaper, and cuddle her doll. This will help her to learn what you will be doing, and will also give her something to play with when you are busy with the baby.
- Talk to your child about what babies do and need. Many children will expect someone to play with, not someone who cries or sleeps most of the time.

On the Day of the Birth

- A daily plan is important for a toddler. Make sure your child knows who will take care of her when you go to the hospital, and try to keep her day as normal as possible. If she'll be staying overnight somewhere, make sure she's been there before and is happy to go.
- If you are planning on having your toddler with you for part or all of your labour, make sure there is a safe, caring adult with you who has the job of looking after your child only. If your child becomes upset or wants to leave, you or your partner cannot help her in the middle of labour or birth because you will need to help each other. Make sure that your child knows and is happy with the person who will care for her.
- Have your child visit the new baby as soon as possible, preferably when no other visitors are there so you can help her with this new experience. Help her to safely hold the baby and talk about how much they look alike or how the baby is looking right up at her.
- You may want to give your toddler a special "birthday gift" that's from the baby.

At Home After the Birth

Don't be surprised if your toddler wants a bottle or to breastfeed, or is wetting his pants if toilet trained. He may ask to have a soother again or to be in the crib to sleep. You may also find you have a new nighttime visitor as your toddler comes to your bed for comfort. Don't worry; this is normal. It is hard to go from being the only child to being an older brother. Let your toddler take these few steps back into babyhood and help him to handle the big change by letting him go back to babyhood for a short time. Praise him for the skills he shows you,

and talk about what he can do that the baby can't yet, like eating with a spoon or telling you what to have for lunch.

A Few Other Ideas on Making a New Baby More Welcome

- Make sure that you spend time with your toddler. Tantrums, whining, or baby habits will not last long when you spend time with your child and let him know that you still love him. This may be as simple as giving him a drink and having him sit beside you or reading a book when you breastfeed, or throwing a soft toy back and forth with your toddler while the baby rests beside you. If there are two parents in the house, take turns spending time with your toddler doing something that is just for him.
- With a new baby in the house you may feel tired and pulled in too many directions at once. Plan how you can look after both yourself and your children. When the baby is sleeping and you're hoping to rest, cuddle up with your toddler and read or nap together. Walks are good for everyone: you'll get exercise, your toddler can see new things, and the baby will get some fresh air. If you have to decide between baking or spending time with your toddler, buy some ready-made breads and go play. This is the time to make things simple.
- Let your child help with the baby care if he wants to. Toddlers can fold diapers, get the baby's towel and washcloth, and help to bathe the baby. Be careful to let your toddler do only the things that are safe. Pinning a diaper, for example, should not be a toddler job. Do not leave a baby alone with a toddler.
- Try not to use the baby as the reason not to do something. Avoid saying *"I can't play with you now because I have to feed the baby."* Instead, say, *"When I've finished feeding the baby I'd like to read you a story."*
- As much as possible, keep bedtime, meals, baths, and as many other little things in your toddler's life the same as they were before the baby arrived. This will help him feel safe and happy as his home changes for the new baby. At night, if possible, have one parent care for the baby while the other helps your toddler to bed.

Child Care Choices

Choosing child care is an important and sometimes hard decision. If you go back to work, it may mean the end of the special time with your child. For some parents it may feel good, since it means that you have time to do some things for yourself again. Whether you need child care for a very small number of hours or full-time (40 hours a week), spend the time needed to find the setting that is right for you and your child.

There are many child-care choices available. Some families have grandparents or other family to look after their children, while others have a babysitter or a nanny to come to their home. Some take their child to a family daycare provider who cares for a small group of children of different ages in their own home. And still others choose group child care at a centre.

Think about what it is that you are looking for or need.

Plan What Will Work for Your Family

- Do you need care full-time, part-time, or for only a few days a month?
- Can you get your child to daycare or does the caregiver need to come to you?
- Do you need care for the same days each week? Or will you need someone at short notice, or someone who can stay at night if necessary, or someone to care for your child on different days each week?
- How many hours of child care do you need each day? Think about travel time to and from daycare.
- Can you find child care close to your workplace?
- How much can you pay? You can contact your local Ministry of Human Resources office (in the blue pages of your phone book) for information about child care subsidies.

Plan What Will Work for Your Child

- Does your child like large groups, small groups, or does he like one-to-one attention?
- Do you think he will be happy at home with one caregiver? Having brothers or sisters at home helps.
- Does your child like going out and having lots of things to do, or does he like quiet times the best?

Children can be happy in many different sorts of child-care settings.

Child Care Outside of Your Home

If you choose child care out of your home, check that the facility is licensed if more than two children (who are not family of the caregiver) are in the group. This is a rule even if the daycare is in a person's own home. A child-care place must meet licensing requirements for the ages and number of children allowed for each caregiver, staff qualifications, space and equipment, criminal record checks, nutrition, smoking, discipline, emergency procedures, and programs and activities.

Centre-based child care and family child-care homes can both offer quality care, so you need to weigh the pros and cons when choosing where you will place your child. For example, in centre-based care, if a caregiver is ill there are others to take her place, and you can feel secure that the daycare will be open. Your child will meet other children of the same age and may make a new friend. If you choose a family child-care provider, the provider *may* have a back-up person arranged for the occasional sick day or holiday.

There are also some things to think about when choosing child care out of your home. The more children in a group, the easier it is to pass on colds and

germs just because there are more children. Also, the days and times that group daycare is open may not be the times you need. Family daycare, since it is run out of a home, may give you early drop off or late pick up if you need it.

Choosing licensed child care, either centre-based or family child care, means that there are regulations and policies in place to help ensure the health, safety, and well-being of your child. If you choose a legally unlicensed facility (one where the caregiver looks after her own children and has no more than two other children not in her family), you will need to satisfy yourself as to its safety and rules.

When choosing a child-care facility, look for one where:

- If they are licensed, the license is where you can see it.
- Visiting your child at any time is easy and you can go into any part of the daycare.
- The caregivers are warm, caring, and help your child to learn.
- There are toys that are safe, fun, and help learning for the children.
- The daycare is clean, has enough light, and is safe.
- You can to talk with the caregivers about your child.
- You are asked what immunizations your child has had (your child's health passport will give you this information), and about any health problems.
- They have car seats for the right age and size of all the children who will be going on trips in the car or van.
- You are asked for the names of people who may pick up your child for you.
- You are asked how the daycare can find you in an emergency and who to contact if you cannot be found.

For more information on selecting a child-care facility, contact your local licensing program in your health region for a copy of the booklet "A Parent's Guide to Selecting Child Care." If you need help in finding the licensing program in your health authority, call Enquiry BC toll-free at 1-800-663-7867. This booklet is also available on the Ministry web site at www.healthplanning.gov.bc.ca

Child Care in Your Home

When you decide to have child care in your home, think about what it means to have a new person in your home on their own with your child and what is important to you. Think about the changes there will be with another person in your home and what things you are private about and how you can feel okay about this. In-home child care may be the right choice for you and your child because your child stays in the place he knows best, with one person to care for him. If your child is ill, he can be comfortable at home and you can still carry on with your work. You will not need to think about travel to child care and the time this takes, so you may have more time to spend with your child in the morning and evening.

With in-home care you may want to plan for your child to visit with other children who are also at home or to go out on trips, e.g., to the library, for story time so that he has a chance to play with other children. Your child will get to know, and will usually grow very attached to, his caregiver and may be upset if and when he or she leaves. You will also need to think about and plan for what you will do if your caregiver doesn't show up, is ill, or leaves without warning. If a family member is the care provider, talk about the things you are looking for in the same way you would with another care provider outside of your family so that they know what you want and how you will bring up any problems you have. This will help to keep a good relationship with that family member.

One way to find in-home care providers is to ask other people with children who they know and like as a care provider, or by calling a placement or nanny agency, or by looking in the paper or bulletin boards, or by calling child-care resource centres. Ask for references and talk with previous parent employers. You can also ask for a criminal record check to be completed and for information on their driving record.

When interviewing care providers, ask questions such as:

- What is their training?
- What recent work experience do they have with children? (Ask about the ages they have worked with, the number of children, years of work, and reason(s) for leaving.)
- What do they feel is important about caring for children? For example, what are their views about discipline, play, toys, nutrition, siblings, activity, television?
- Do they have first aid or infant CPR training? If so, do they have a current certificate? How do they handle an emergency?
- Do they have religious practices or holidays that may be different from your own?

Talk about what you expect them to do when working with your child, and what you agree upon, and record this in a written and signed contract.

Things to think about that should be covered in the contract:

- Hours and days of work, and overtime pay if this needs to be part of the plan or some other agreement.
- What you will pay, how often and when you will pay, sick time, paid holidays, pay by the hour or daily.

- What is expected in terms of meals, e.g., are they to provide their own food, or will they share meals with your child?
- Expected activities with your child, such as meals, baths, walks, play and teaching, or trips to the park.
- Expected activities in the home, such as housekeeping, preparing meals, laundry, or grocery shopping.
- If they will be driving with your child, what seats they will use, who will provide them, and what is their driving ability and experience?

If someone provides child care in your home and is not employed by an agency, you are his or her employer. When you are an employer, the following laws may apply to you.

Federal Laws

Depending on how many hours your caregiver works, the federal government may consider you an employer. Contact your local Revenue Canada office to learn how the Income Tax Act, Canada Pension Plan, and Employment Insurance Act apply.

Provincial Laws

Again, depending on how many hours your caregiver works, you may have to comply with the Workers' Compensation Act. Contact the Workers' Compensation Board to find out what this means to your situation. You should know that all employers must comply with the BC Human Rights Act.

For information on choosing quality child care, contact your local licensing office or Child Care Resource and Referral program (CCRR). For information about child-care subsidies, contact your local Ministry of Community, Aboriginal and Women's Services office.

For more information about child care, check this web site: www.mcaws.gov.bc.ca.

Once you have decided on the child care, talk about it with your child. Visit the daycare with your child or spend some time with the child-care provider in your home so your child can learn about where he will be and who he will be with when he is being cared for.

Introducing Your Toddler to a New Child-Care Setting

- If your toddler is being cared for outside of your home, visit the daycare and have him meet the caregiver(s) before you plan to leave him there.
- On his first day, stay for as long as you need to to see that your toddler gets used to the setting. Make sure that when you leave, his care provider is able to give him attention. Let him know that you will return with comments such as, *"I'll come back after you wake up from your nap."*
- At home, talk with interest about the child-care setting and the care provider. Remind your toddler about any toys, activities, or other children that he had fun with.
- You may want to get him a special lunch bag or rubber boots for the daycare so that he can take something from home with him.

When You Leave

- Tell your child, whether he is a toddler or a baby, that you are leaving—don't just disappear when he starts to play. Although it may seem harder at the time, your child will become sure that you will tell him about changes, and will be less anxious. Goodbyes are easier in the long run if he has a sense of trust and if the fact that you come and go is something he understands.
- Develop a ritual around your departure with your child. *"I'll watch you go down the slide and then it's time for me to go."* Say and do the same things each time you leave.
- Make sure that your toddler's care provider is able to help him separate from you by giving him one-to-one attention as you are leaving.
- Call if any plans change or if you'll be late. This can help to keep your child from worrying or being afraid that you won't come back.

When You Return

- Give your child special attention. *"I'm so glad to see you. Could you show me the truck that you like?"*
- Talk to your child about what he did while you were away. Tell him what you were doing.
- Ask the care provider about your child's day. Find out what they did while you were gone so that you can talk about anything special that happened or any concerns. Some daycares keep

a written note each day so you can check on their day and activities.

If Your Child Seems Unhappy with the Child Care

- Don't hesitate to ask the care provider for information about your child and the daycare; for example, how long they slept, what they ate, or how the children are playing together. Talk about any problems with the care provider.
- Be aware that there may be a "honeymoon phase." Your child may seem to be happy for several weeks and then unhappy.
- Call the care provider to see how your child is doing or drop in and observe.
- Find out whether your child stays upset after you have gone. Ask another parent to watch your child, or wait and listen outside the door.
- If your child is old enough to talk, ask him what he likes and what he doesn't like about the child care. Small children may be upset by the behaviour of another child or frightened by a scary picture in a book.
- If your child continues to be unhappy, think about other child-care options.

Moving to a New Home

Even in the best of circumstances, moving house is usually stressful and tiring for everyone. Take heart that your toddler is at an age where she is not likely to be as upset about leaving friends and schools as an older child may be. If you keep her routines the same and favourite people and things nearby, the move will be fine.

Tips on Preparing Your Child for a Move:

- Don't surprise your toddler. Clearly and simply explain where and when you will be moving.
- Read stories about moving, and play with moving toys such as boxes, trucks, or planes.
- If possible, take your child to visit your new home before you move in.
- If you are moving to a new neighbourhood, visit it with your child first. Visit parks, pools, libraries, or any other place that may be interesting.
- Give her a box where she can put her toys and other treasures. This also helps her to understand

that you aren't throwing things out when they are packed away.

- Look for signs of stress. Your child may stop using the toilet if she is toilet trained or go back to wanting a soother, or teddy.
- Don't make this a time to get rid of loved objects and furniture or clothes—do this either before the move or well after. As well, don't use the move as a time to switch from the crib to a bed or to "lose" your child's bottle or soother. Too many changes will cause problems.
- If possible, pack up your child's room last and unpack it first. Put your child's bedroom in a pattern that will seem familiar to her.
- The most important thing you can do to make a move less stressful for everyone is to give extra attention and love to your toddler.

Separation or Divorce

▶ **Q: "Our two-year-old seems to have taken our separation very hard. She's sucking her thumb and twirling her hair any chance she gets, and has started asking to breastfeed, which we had stopped a year ago. I don't know what to do. My ex and I fight every time we see each other, and we're just not doing the best we can for our daughter."**

▶ **A:** This is a very big change for your family. Your world as you know it will need to be organized differently and you will need to develop different supports. With a divorce, children are usually very upset and need you to behave in a calm and matter-of-fact way even though what is happening is very stressful.

Living in a home with constant fighting or unhappiness is not healthy for children, nor does it provide a good example for healthy relationships. If this is what is happening in your family, talk to an adult you trust who can help you. A single-parent home, co-parenting, or a two-home family may be better for your child. No matter how messy your breakup is, try to keep your children out of the discussion and tension. They need to feel safe and secure, now more than ever. You may have strong feelings about your ex-partner, but remember that these feelings are *yours* and not your child's. She still needs to know that Mom and Dad are the greatest people in the world and will be there for her. Young

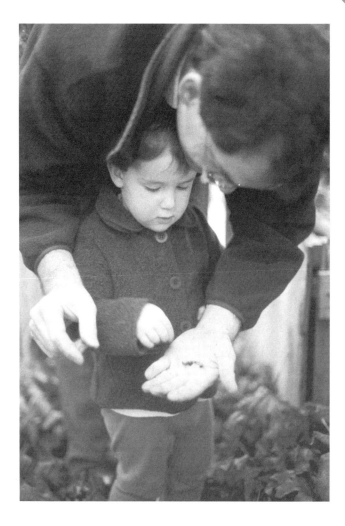

children are not able to understand the details of your problems. These are all adult concerns.

Tips on Communicating with Your Ex-partner
- Children learn about communication and relationships by watching their parents and other important adults. Be very aware that your child is learning from you as you work with your ex-partner.
- Be aware of where your child is when you are talking with or about your ex-partner. If your child can hear you, make sure that anything you say, as well as your tone of voice, will not be upsetting to your child.
- You don't need to like your ex-partner to be able to parent well, but you do need to work well with him or her. Try to think of yourselves as business partners or co-workers who have the job of caring for and supporting children. Even if you are communicating through written notes or phone messages at first, this is a good start,

and will help to make sure that information about your child is available. Do not use your child to share information between you. Keep her at a distance from your dealings with each other if possible.

- If you are having difficulty being calm around your ex-partner, try to arrange visits for your child through someone else, such as a friend or family member. If your child is in daycare, another way is to have one parent drop off, and another pick up.
- Try to think about it not as reducing your child's life by one parent, but as starting a new way of parenting, with two homes and no fighting.

When talking with your child about your separation, give her time to ask questions and get used to the idea. Tell her simply and clearly what is happening. Saying that Mom and Dad are not happy together and will be happier if they live apart is much more understandable than going into adult problems such as responsibility or trust. Be sure your child understands that she is not the reason for the separation. Toddlers are very self-centred and may believe that they are the cause of their parents' unhappiness. Be prepared to have the same discussions over and over. It takes toddlers a long time to understand these changes.

Tips on Helping Your Child Cope with Your Separation

- Let your child know often you will not leave her on her own. Just because Mom and Dad don't live together any more doesn't change the fact

that she has two parents who love her very much. Make more time to care for your child, not less.

- Let your child talk happily about her mommy or daddy, without any disapproving comments from you. Children can become stressed trying to remember with whom and when they can talk about their feelings or events in their lives without making a parent upset. Try to keep your comments neutral and calm. *"I'm glad to hear you had fun with Daddy today."* Or *"I like how Mommy did your hair today. It's pretty."*
- Be prepared for angry reactions or difficult behaviours such as tantrums, thumb sucking, going back to diapers, or problems in toilet training. Toddlers will often respond unhappily to changes in their routines or stress in their homes (see page 84 for information on dealing with change in a toddler's life). Be tolerant of your toddler's behaviours. With extra love and support, these reactions will not last long.
- When your child stays with one parent away from his main home, make sure that he has a place for leaving toys, blankets, pyjamas, and other things that make this new home "his." Keep his routines and way of doing things as regular as possible, maintaining such things as bedtime stories, bath times, and favourite foods. These small adjustments will help him feel more secure while he adjusts to the changes in his life.

Most experts recommend that you find an understanding friend, family member, or counsellor who can help you deal with the emotions you may be experiencing and to discuss ways to help your child.

For further reading, see *Mom's House, Dad's House* by Isolina Ricci.

Talking About Death with Your Child

Very young children are just beginning to understand that even though something is out of sight it still exists, and have little to no understanding of time and when and how something is final. You may be heartbroken about a death in the family, but your toddler may hear what you have to say and then simply go and play with little to no reaction. This doesn't mean that she didn't love or care for the person who died.

It means that she does not understand how final death is. You may also find that your toddler reacts with tears, anger, or fear that someone else (or even she) may die.

If you have a death in your family or of a beloved friend, don't keep it a secret from your child. She will know that something is wrong in the family, and will be more afraid of what it could be if you don't talk to her. When talking with your child, use simple terms that she can understand, such as *"Grandma was very sick and died last night. She won't be here with us any more."* Your child, if old enough, will most likely want to know where Grandma is. Depending on your religious beliefs, you can say *"She's in heaven now with God"* or *"She's in a safe place until tomorrow, when she will be buried in the church yard."* Keep your explanations simple and non-frightening, and allow your toddler to express her feelings, whatever they may be. Give details only if you are asked for them.

Before There Is a Death
- Take opportunities to talk to your child about life and death. The garden, the changing seasons, and the death of an insect all provide opportunities to show children that death is a part of life.
- Be truthful and straightforward about death. Children often ask difficult questions, such as *"Will you die? Will I die?"* It's important to try to answer as honestly as possible without creating new fears for your child. *"Yes, we all die, but Mommy and Daddy won't die for a very long time and neither will you."*

When a Loved One or a Pet Dies
- Include your child in your grief. It is important to let your child know that feeling sad and showing grief are normal when a loved one dies. Let your child know that painful feelings are part of living and that, over time, the pain will decrease. *"Sometimes we feel sad because sad things happen. We'll feel better after a while."*
- If you use expressions like *"Grandpa's gone away"* or *"Grandpa's gone to sleep,"* this may confuse your child as she waits for Grandpa to wake up or return, and may start a fear of sleep or travelling.
- This is an important time to keep daily activities the same to help your child keep her sense of security and comfort in knowing what to expect each day (see page 84 for information on helping your child cope with change in her life).
- Keep thoughts of the person or animal alive by talking about them or by looking at pictures. If your child doesn't show an interest, don't push this at her, since some children feel loss by refusing to talk about the person or look at their picture.

Think about how your child might feel and what she might be afraid of. If you notice that your child has a fear of being away from you after the death of her grandmother, she may be showing you that she is afraid that you won't come back, just as her grandmother won't come back. Extra love, attention, and support will help your toddler to go through the many feelings and fears.

▶ **Q: "Should we take our three-year-old to my brother's funeral? She was close to her uncle, but I think it may upset her too much."**

▶ **A:** Think about what your child will learn from attending the funeral. She will be able to share with her family the chance to say goodbye to her uncle. She will also be with her family, usually the most secure place, at a stressful and sad time. The negative aspects of going are that she may see people she trusts and needs to help her (yourself, Grandma, or Grandpa) break down or lose control, which could be very frightening for her. If the casket is open, do you want her to remember her uncle this way or do you want her to think of him when he was alive? Your child can stay at home with a trusted caregiver and share with the family gathering after, or attend part of the funeral, leaving if and when emotions rise. You could have your own special ceremony with her another time by bringing flowers to the grave or by saying goodbye in another way.

CHAPTER 5

Making Your Child's World Safer

Home and community are places for a toddler to develop a sense of safety and of being loved and cared for. They are also places for your child to learn about others and share joy and sadness, and to develop a sense of well-being. The first year of life is the time when your child develops a sense of trust.

In the toddler years the brain of a young child is using the events that happen each day—experiences—to organize thought processes through what is thought to be "brain connections." These connections are the building blocks or beginning points for new skills to develop. Researchers are beginning to understand that the brain makes connections very quickly when children are young and keeps these early connections as the beginning of future skills. These important connections can be built later, but then the process may take longer and more work.

Children Are Greatly Affected by Violence

Watching or experiencing violence can change a child's ability to learn about and reach out to adults and other children. Researchers are beginning to understand that if your child is around violence often, or feels worried about threats of violence, his brain keeps this as a "pathway" for future use and he will learn to see violence as the usual way to act. The more he is around violence or feeling the threat of violence, it seems the more quickly a child will act out (fight response) or run in fear (flight response) or shut down (disassociation).

Don't be fooled into thinking that your child is not upset by violence because he doesn't show you he is upset each time he experiences violence. At first he may cry to get your attention. If this does not help, he may soon shut down and become silent. Although he does not continue to tell or show you that he's upset, the child continues to have the same physical and emotional reactions. Some emerging research is showing that a child who is around violence a lot may always feel upset or anxious, even though he doesn't show or tell you that is how he is feeling. Think about how tiring it would be to always be on edge and worried that you or someone you love and depend on may be frightened or hurt at any moment.

Sometimes parents feel quite helpless to do anything about the violence in their homes. There is help. **If you find yourself in violent situations, you must make a move to protect both you and your child right away!** Talk with your crisis line, local women's shelter, child protection social worker, doctor, or public health nurse. See page 118 for more information on further resources. Anyone who has a reason to believe that a child is in a violent or abusive situation must report this to the closest child protection social worker. If you know that you have had violent experiences in your life, it might help you to learn more about identifying violent situations early if you talk about this with a community counsellor or a social worker.

Making Your Home Safe for Your Toddler

Toddlers explore their world by climbing, touching, tasting, licking, and chewing on almost anything. Some things your toddler may put in his mouth can be very harmful or even cause death. As your child grows, keep thinking about safety and take steps to make sure your home is safe for an exploring toddler. You will then be able to relax a little as well.

Accidents often happen when a parent is surprised by a new skill their child has developed or is developing. In the first three years you will be surprised at how quickly your child learns and will show you new skills—and how much you have to watch and know to keep up! Your toddler may not have been able to climb onto the couch yesterday—but you may find him up on the couch and carefully climbing the bookcase today. It only takes a moment for a child who knows what he wants to do to learn a new skill.

Children under three years do not understand danger and do not remember *"No"* when they are busy exploring their worlds. Therefore, it is important for you to make your home as safe as you can (childproof) and to develop safer ways of working in your home *before* your toddler surprises you by getting hurt.

General Home Safety Tips

☑ Check your smoke detectors or alarms every month, by pressing the test button, to make sure that the batteries are working or, if the detector is wired into the electrical system, that the alarm itself is working. The Office of the Fire Commissioner and most fire departments recommend that you replace the batteries once a year or, for extended life batteries, according to manufacturer's instructions. Batteries should be replaced when the smoke alarm makes a chirping sound.

☑ Know basic first aid, including what to do if someone is choking, and what to do if a child stops breathing (Cardio Pulmonary Resuscitation or CPR). Contact your local St. John Ambulance, Red Cross, or community centre to sign up for classes on these important skills.

☑ Keep emergency numbers by each phone in your house, including 911, and the numbers for poison control and your doctor. You may know these numbers, but other caregivers may not.

☑ Set the water temperature in your hot water tank at 49°C (120°F) to prevent burns.

☑ Remove leaded mini-blinds from your home, and make sure your child cannot reach dangling cords.

☑ Drawstrings on children's outfits are very dangerous. It is recommended that parents remove all hood and neck strings from children's outerwear, including jackets and sweatshirts, so the drawstrings will not get caught on the corner posts of a crib or on playground equipment. This could strangle a child. Many manufacturers have stopped making clothes with hood or neck strings, and have put on snaps to prevent this type of accident.

☑ Make sure bookcases, television cabinets, or other furniture that could be pulled down onto a child, or may become dangerous in an earthquake, will not fall over, (e.g., screw them to the wall with safety screws).

☑ Keep a fire extinguisher in the kitchen, away from the stove. Keep it near a door to the outside so you can use it and leave if necessary.

General Childproofing Tips

One way to start childproofing is to start by looking at your home through your child's eyes. This means *hit the floor!* Crawl around on your hands and knees and look at the kinds of things that your child might be curious about or interested in. Electrical plugs or lamps that could be easily pulled over should be covered up, moved, or removed.

• *"I almost cried when I saw him with a cigarette butt in his mouth!"* Toddlers learn by watching and doing, and will try to do what you do. Keep this in mind, and be sure that whatever you do in front of your child, you also want her to do. It is much safer if your child does not watch you (or other important adults) take pills or medicine, put diaper pins or bobby pins in your mouth, or smoke.

- *Balloons are not toys for young children*, although children will play with them and many people think they are toys. Always supervise your toddler when balloons are around. Never let children chew on pieces of balloons or balloons that do not have air in them. When throwing balloons away, make sure that the balloon is out of reach completely (not just loose in the garbage, where a child can still get at it). Balloons are one of the biggest choking threats for children of all ages. A child's airway can be blocked completely by a balloon or piece of balloon very quickly. It is best for young children not to play with balloons at all. If you must use them, help your child to learn that they are for looking at only.

- *"When our son started walking, the coffee table was a magnet—he ran into it every time he moved."* Sharp edges on furniture or fireplaces can injure your child when he runs into them or falls onto them. Overhanging edges from a counter or table may be above, or at a toddler's eye level.

Soften these edges by putting homemade or store-bought corner guards or cushioned strips on the corners and edges.

- *"After watching me plug things in and make noise, I saw my one-and-a-half-year-old trying to poke a paper clip into an outlet."* Put outlet covers on all electrical outlets you are not using.

- Smoking—the best thing you can do for your child is to have a smoke-free home. Do not smoke, or let someone else smoke, when your child is around. Also, make sure that your child cannot touch ashtrays, matches, lighters, or cigarettes.

- *"My two-year-old was into Grandma's purse and was trying to open her heart pills!"* Make sure that your purse, and anyone else's purse, is out of reach and high up. Purses can contain coins, small mints, and medications that can harm your child.

- *"The stairs made me a nervous wreck!"* At about the age of two, your toddler will start going up and down stairs on his own. Going up stairs is a skill that may be learned easily and well, but make sure you watch. Be there to help anyway. Going down is when your child can easily be hurt. She will still be very unsteady and inexperienced. **Do not take the gates away from the bottom and the top of the stairs until your child shows you that she can use the stairs easily all the time.** Teach your child to go up and down facing the stairs. Also keep toys off the stairs, and put away any loose carpets that are on them. See page 100 for more information on gates.

- Toddlers may not be steady on their feet and they fall easily. Young children should not carry breakable things such as glass when they are walking, nor should they walk with suckers or Popsicles in their mouths. Glass doors should have decals, cutouts, or your child's artwork at your child's eye level so that he'll see them. Running near glass doors is dangerous.

- *"My child loves to play in the recycling cupboard. We called it her office."* Be careful with your recycle bin: your toddler may want to chew on the newspapers, which contain ink that can hurt her if she eats large amounts. Your child may want to play with magazines or brochures and may suck on them, so keep those away from her, too. The bright colours in the magazines (which toddlers love) can contain lead and be harmful to your child. Tin cans may also be in your recycle bin and the sharp edges will cut your child.

- *"I had to move the soaps up, too—she kept trying to 'do like Mommy'."* Keep laundry soaps and other cleaning products on a high shelf and locked up. Your child may put them in her mouth. Soaps and cleaners are very dangerous; even hair shampoo can be dangerous.

- *Fires are fascinating!* Fireplaces or inserts should be completely screened when a fire is blazing or at a low burn and even if a fire has gone out. The fireplace glass and other hot surfaces are really dangerous and can burn a child's hands very quickly.

- A chest freezer can be a danger for the older toddler, who can fall in when reaching for frozen treats. Be sure to keep your freezer locked and store the key where your child cannot get to it.

- *"She thinks she's Tarzan, always trying to swing on something."* Cords on blinds and drapes must be tied up where your child cannot reach them, even when she climbs on the furniture.

Tie cords on blinds and drapes up out of reach or clip them up, cut them off or fasten them high and to the side.

- *"It only took two minutes for him to turn over the laundry basket and climb up on our dresser. I found him leaning out of the window looking at the birds."* Make sure that you have window locks on all upstairs windows and that the doors to rooms that contain things a young child should not have are kept locked at all times.

- If you have an older home that may have been painted with lead-based paint, take paint chips or flakes and have them tested. Do not sand until you know there is no lead in the paint; it will create lead dust. (Contact your local Environmental Health Department about how you can remove old paint safely.)

- Don't think that a safety latch on a cupboard will protect your child from harmful substances completely. **Safety latches are designed to make the opening of cupboards more difficult for children, not impossible.** Some children love a challenge and will be determined to find a way into a place they know is off limits. Dangerous products must be kept locked away.

- A number of other safety ideas that will help you keep your toddler safe can be found in *Baby's Best Chance, "Protecting Your Baby from Harm."*

did you know?

Eighty percent of all injuries to babies and toddlers happen in their own homes. They most often involve falls, poisoning, scalds, burns, choking, and drowning.

In the Bathroom

"One day we were all busy in the bathroom when we noticed our toddler 'brushing her hair' with my razor. I had put it on the edge of the bathtub."

Many things in the bathroom, such as soaps or shampoo, smell nice—so nice that your toddler may want to taste or drink them. He also watches you every day as you put on makeup, shave, or generally "play with *your* toys" in this special room. This is very interesting to a toddler and he will try to do what you do! Most bathrooms have low cupboards under the sink that may have dangerous things in them, so lock these cupboards. Most toddlers like the toilet. They can fall into it head first and not be able to get out—yes, a child could drown. Leave the toilet lid down and make sure that when your toddler is in the bathroom, you are there too.

It's important to check out the bathroom and make it safe for your child. Think about the following questions:

☑ Are you always with your child when she's in the bathroom?

☑ Is the hot water heater set to 49°C (120°F)?

☑ If you live in an apartment, do you have an anti-scald guard on your sink, bathtub spouts, and showerhead?

☑ Are hair dryers, electric razors, and curling irons unplugged and put away after each use?

☑ Are sharp things like razors, scissors, and nail files in a drawer with a safety lock or kept out of reach?

☑ Are all medications, cosmetics, powders, and perfumes kept in a high or locked cabinet out of the reach of children?

☑ Are items like bottles of mouthwash, nail polish, nail polish remover, hair spray, hair dye, and shampoo kept locked out of the reach of children?

☑ Are bathroom cleansers and deodorizers locked up and out of reach?

☑ Are there non-skid treads or is there a rubber bathmat on the bottom of the bathtub?

☑ Is the lid on the toilet seat kept closed?

☑ Can the bathroom door be easily unlocked from the outside?

If you cannot answer "*Yes*" to all of these questions, you have some childproofing work to do.

Kitchen Safety

"*My son loved to play in the kitchen cupboards and I had to keep moving him away from these over and over, so I decided to work with him. We gave him his own small cupboard, away from the stove, with all my plastic containers in it. I would put a new toy, or something new I was hoping he would learn about, in the cupboard every few days. At first, when he was a*

year old, it was big blocks he would stack, or he would put Cheerios into a container. Then, when he was about two, I put easy puzzles in there or jars with small toys inside them so that he would take the lids off. Now that he's three, he knows that a one-cup measure and a half-cup measure are different and loves helping me with baking. I can do my chores more easily with him busy, and he is happy right beside me."

All children love to be where you are and to be part of what is happening in their home. In many houses the kitchen is the action place. This can be the most dangerous room in the house and your child will be spending a lot of time there—so ask yourself these questions to make your life easier and your toddler's life safer:

☑ Are pot handles turned to the middle or inside of the stove, and not over another element?

☑ Do you use the back burners of the stove for boiling and simmering and the front for simmering only? It is even better if you try to cook using only the back burners.

☑ Some experts suggest that you make a safety zone in front of the stove, using a skid-proof rug, and teach your child that the "rug zone" is off limits.

☑ Are small appliances unplugged and placed out of reach? Remember to unplug them from the wall first—never from the appliance. A child can be seriously burned if he puts the cord end into his mouth.

☑ Do you have your garbage inside a latched cupboard or in a bin with a lid that is hard to take off? Toddlers love to take everything apart and taste it, even garbage.

☑ Are knives, scissors, and other sharp items put away in a drawer that your child cannot get into?

☑ Are vitamins, medications, and household cleaners in locked cabinets?

☑ Are plastic bags tied in a knot and kept out of reach? If your child puts one on over her head, she could stop breathing.

☑ Are small foods that could cause choking, such as beans or nuts, kept out of reach?

☑ Does your child's high chair have a wide base so it cannot tip over?

☑ Is the high chair or booster chair far enough away from appliances, windows, blind cords, mirrors, and sharp corners of counters?

☑ Does the high chair have a safety strap that fits between your child's legs and a waist belt that is easy to use and kept in good condition?

☑ If you use a tablecloth, is it safely away from your child's reach (to keep her from pulling it)?

☑ Do you keep the dishwasher locked and the soap container empty until ready for use?

You should be able to answer "*Yes*" to all these questions. If not, you have some child safety work to do.

Remember that most injuries happen:
- In your own home.
- When you're doing something else (such as talking on the telephone).
- When you don't know your child has learned a new skill.
- When either you or your child is tired, such as around dinnertime.

Equipment in Your Home

Safe Toys

Toys are an important part of playtime as children grow and develop. It's important that the toys you have are safe and that an adult who knows about safety is around when a child is playing. This is especially true for children under three years of age who are very curious but not yet experienced in safe play. One half of all toy-related deaths among children involve choking. Many of these choking deaths happen when children try to swallow marbles, small balls, small parts or parts that are broken, or objects that are not really toys.

No matter what the age or developmental stage of your child, follow these basic rules:
- Throw away any wrappings or bags that come with new toys immediately; they can suffocate your child.
- Never use plastic/styrofoam egg cartons and packing material (expanded polystyrene) as a toy. If your child breathes these in or pushes them into her nose or ear, or swallows these things, they can stay in place and cannot be found by an X-ray. If swallowed, this material will not be broken down by digestive juices in the stomach.
- Check toys often. A broken toy may become a choking hazard, or have sharp edges that can cut your child. Check toys for loose seams where stuffing can come out, or sewn-on eyes or ears that have become loose. Check for wear often and fix or throw out broken toys right away.
- Toys that sound too loud for you, such as horns or sirens, will be too loud for your child's young ears and can cause lasting damage.
- Make sure you or another adult is watching when any toys with batteries are played with. When not in use, the batteries or toys with batteries should be stored where your child cannot get them. A battery can be swallowed or breathed in if it is a small one. It is very dangerous for a child to chew on batteries because they will leak.
- Keep toys that are not being used in a box out of the way to prevent falls, toy damage, or use without a trusted adult around during play. Also, check toy-box lids and pad them so pinching or bruises won't happen if the lid is dropped. Make sure toy boxes have air holes just in case your child climbs in the box when you are not looking.

- A string, cord, or ribbon any longer than 15 cm (6 in.) can wrap around a child's neck and cut off breathing (strangulation). Cut these cords short or take them off toys before letting your child play with the toys. Put the cords safely away or throw them out. Do not let your child play with audiotapes. Children love to unwind them, and again their breathing could be cut off. Don't leave any ropes, such as a skipping rope, where your child can get it.

- Make sure you can wash your toys. Check the care tag on stuffed toys to ensure that they are marked "Washable." Unwashed stuffed toys can be germ catchers. Many stuffed toys can be put in a pillowcase with the top knotted and put through the washer and dryer with good results.

- Give your child well-made toys. The toys last longer and stand up to hard play. They can be safer because they usually will not splinter or break into small pieces that can be swallowed or breathed in.

- Any toy that fits completely into your child's mouth is too small for him to play with. Check that your child is not squashing a larger toy (such as playdough or a sponge) into a smaller size and putting it into his mouth. Anything that can pass down the middle of a toilet paper roll is too small for a toddler to play with unless you are playing too and watching for danger.

- If a toy is painted, make sure the finish is non-toxic and cannot peel.

- Always look for safety information on a toy's warning label, and choose toys that have a label that says the toy is in the age and developmental stage of your child.

- When your toddler is playing on a riding toy or tricycle, watch carefully and make sure this play is in a safe place. Toddlers generally do not have the skills to use a trike well, so many injuries occur when they are using these toys. Wait and watch.

- Do not allow a young child to use a trampoline. They're dangerous for young children and an injury is often very serious.

- If your child sucks or chews teethers or rattles made of soft vinyl, make sure the labels say they are made without PVC. PVC is a chemical that makes vinyl softer and can be harmful to young children.

▶ **Q: "We have a seven-year-old and an 18-month-old. How are we going to make sure the younger one is safe when his brother has all these small toys?"**

▶ **A:** This is a common problem in families with more than one child. Get your older child to help you with this problem. Talk to him about being the big boy in the house and about the job he has to help keep his little brother safely away from his toys. (He may even be happy that he doesn't have to share them.) If he is old enough to be in his room by himself, he can shut the door to his room when he plays with his toys. If you want to watch, then a safety gate could be useful in his doorway to keep your toddler out during playtime. Store the big-boy toys where your toddler can't get at them and be extra careful when they are out. Small parts can roll away and be hidden from sight until a crawling toddler finds them. If your older child is playing with his toys, show your toddler books or toys for him.

Gates

- Gates can help protect your child from stairs or rooms that are not child safe. Get an approved gate before you think you need it. Remember toddlers often try new activities before you are ready and often when you are not expecting a new skill. In choosing a gate, remember:

- Accordion-style gates are not recommended because the large V-shaped openings along the top and/or the diamond-shaped openings along the sides can be large enough to trap a child's head.

- Pressure gates can be pushed over quite easily. They should only be used between rooms or in hallways.

- Swing gates attach to the wall with hinges on one side, but open on the other side (like a door). This is the only gate that is safe for the top of the stairs and it is a good idea to have one on the bottom of the stairs too.

- Never try to increase the height of a gate by putting it up off the floor. Your child may try to crawl under it.

- If you are buying a new or used gate, make sure that every wooden, metal, or plastic part is smoothly finished and free of splinters,

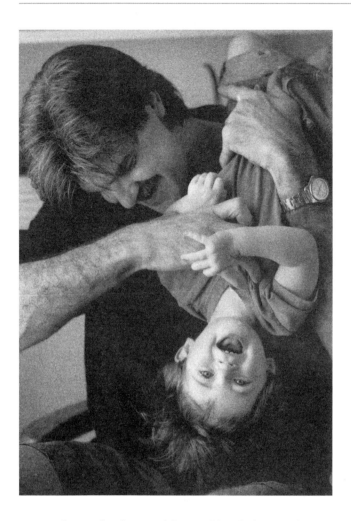

- Buy a high chair built with a wide base, strong tray locks and sturdy construction. Be careful—older chairs may not have all the safety features of the newer models.
- Safety restraining straps should always be used. There should be two straps: one around your child's waist and one between his legs.
- A fold-away high chair may take up less room, but make sure that the locking devices are in place each time you set it up.
- Make sure that your child's hands, arms, and legs cannot get caught in any moving parts when changing the chair or tray position.
- Don't let older children climb into the chair, since this can tip it over.

cracks, and other problems. Check for a safety-approved label and look at product safety recall information.

Table Time

Safe seating for the age and size of your child will make mealtimes easier and more fun for the whole family. There are three basic seating choices for toddlers: the high chair, booster seat, and hook-on chair. There is, of course, always the option of your lap, but you will want your hands free for your own meal and your child will want freedom. Think about the following safety tips:

High Chairs

The most common injuries in high chairs happen when the chair is tipped over by your toddler when he's pushing off from a solid piece of furniture, wall, or table, or when your child crawls out and falls or slips under the tray and gets tangled in the safety straps.

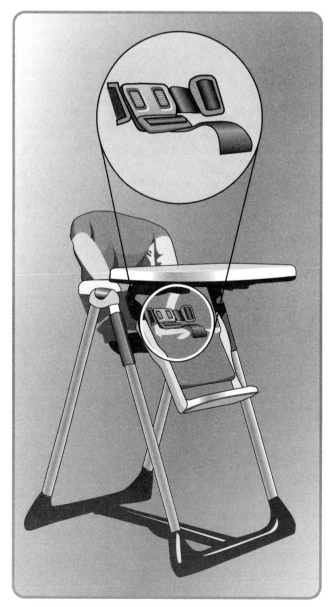

Booster Seats

Booster seats are useful when your child grows out of her high chair but is still too small for an adult chair. Boosters are placed on your regular kitchen chair and are held in place with a safety belt that normally goes around the back of the chair. Some boosters also have a safety or restraining strap to hold your toddler in the seat. These straps should be made to fit comfortably around your child so she is firmly in the seat. Crossed safety straps should be placed low enough that they do not or cannot reach your child's neck, even if she slips down in her seat. A toddler must not be left alone in a booster seat since your child can still move around and fall, and would need help if this happened.

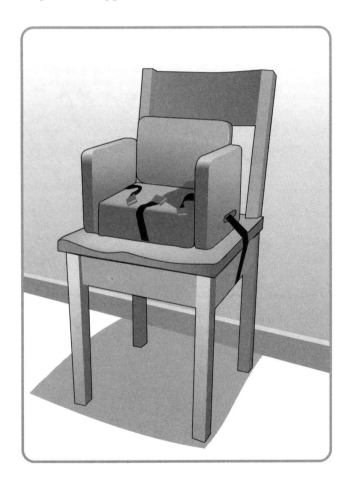

Hook-on Chairs

Hook-on chairs attach to the side of your table. They do not have legs, and are not supported by a chair. A high chair is usually safer than a hook-on seat because a hook-on seat can tip a lightweight table over or be moved by an active toddler. If you do use a hook-on, remember:

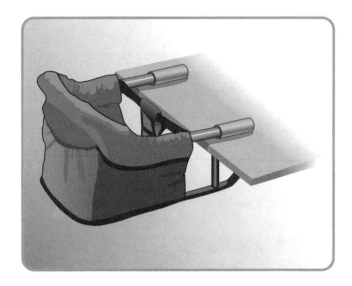

- Attach the hook-on only to a strong table that is not shaky.
- Do not use a hook-on if your child is over 13.5 kilograms (30 pounds) or is very active.
- Do not place the hook-on near a table leg, since your child can push against the table leg to loosen the chair and push it off the table.
- Always be with your child if he is in a hook-on seat.

Beds and Cribs

When to move your child out of her crib and into a big bed is a child, parent, and family decision. Some three-year-olds are still happily sleeping in a crib while some 18-month-olds really want to climb out. You need to know and watch for signs that your toddler is ready to move to a bed. If your toddler is climbing or trying really hard to climb out of the crib, they may soon fall out of the crib. It's time to make the move.

When moving your child to a bed, think about:
- Putting safety rails on both sides of the bed, even if one side is against the wall. Little heads can slide between the bed and wall.
- Moving the bed away from windows, heat sources, draperies, or anything else your child can hurt herself with, since she now has a new climbing tool in her room.
- Putting plush carpets, pillows, or quilts on the floor by the bed, just in case your toddler rolls out. (Most rails don't run the full length of the bed.)

- If your child doesn't seem ready to sleep in a regular bed, toddler beds let you use your crib mattress and are closer to the floor than a regular single bed.
- Bunk beds are not safe for a toddler.

If your child is still in a crib:
- Children under a year should not use a pillow.
- Move the mattress to its lowest position when your child is able to sit up.
- A crib should not contain pillows, bumper pads, or large stuffed animals. This helps reduce the risk of Sudden Infant Death Syndrome or other safety problems, and removes the chance that your child can use them to climb out and fall.

Walkers

Baby walkers with wheels have not been sold in Canada since 1989 because they are very, very dangerous and can tip over, roll down stairs, or fall into a pool. A young child can also reach things like dangling cords and hot, heavy, or poisonous items from a walker. If you have an activity centre that does not move (without wheels), make sure you put it in a safe place where your child can't reach dangerous objects while playing in it.

Poisons in the Home

Most Homes Have 250 Poisons. Where Are Yours?
Children, especially young children, explore with their mouths. They also do not know about or understand the same warning signs as adults do and may not understand that a substance is harmful or toxic. Also, remember that what is okay for an adult may be harmful or toxic to a child.

A child's sense of smell and taste is just beginning to develop, so a child will still put a bad-tasting or -smelling substance into his mouth. Both younger and older children—even teenagers—may not know that a substance is harmful and will taste it to try it out. Children who have tasted poison once may explore more with their mouths and for longer than other toddlers, so are more likely to do it again. It may take a child a very long time to learn about safety, so put the many poisonous things in your home in a locked place and keep the key in a safe place that only you know about and can get at. Do not expect a child to "learn a lesson." Children will often do the same thing again and again because they learn by practising. You must make sure that they do not have the chance to practise dangerous things. You must make your home as safe as possible.

did you know?

Most poisonings occur at the busiest times of the day: dinner hour, when everyone is busy with other things; and between 11 a.m. and noon.

Poison-proofing Tips

"Childproofing your home is an ongoing process. Just like the laundry, it's never done!"

- Children learn and remember which containers hold their food, and do not have the sense of taste or smell to know the difference between what can be eaten and what is not for eating. Because of this, never put or store anything else but food in food containers. **This means that non-food or poisonous things must not be put in food containers.** Don't, for example, put cleaning liquid in a juice bottle or pop bottle or powdered soap in a pickle jar. Another reason for using original containers: if a poisoning happens, the label on the original container lists ingredients and may include emergency treatment information.
- If your child has swallowed any harmful product, be sure to take the container with you to the hospital so that the doctors know what ingredients are involved.
- Never mix household chemicals together. Some mixtures can produce harmful gases.
- Lock any and all poisonous substances out of sight and out of reach of toddlers and older children. Young children are very curious and determined, and can often get to dangerous things by using stools, chairs, and even toys to help in climbing to or reaching forbidden items. Remember that safety latches may only slow down a toddler, not keep him out.
- Be sure to take all poisonous houseplants out of your house and watch for these when you are visiting other homes. For a list of poisonous plants, contact your local Poison Control Centre, listed in the front page of your phone book.
- Buy products in childproof packaging whenever possible and check that the child-resistant safety cap is working. This packaging will still not keep out a child (it will only slow him down at best) and many children, as they grow and develop, can get into them. Some children have even chewed off childproof caps. Childproof or not, store them high up in a locked place.
- When you have visitors, make sure they store their handbags and briefcases in a safe place. Often people will carry medications wrapped in tissues, small bags, or daily pill containers.

- Never leave alcoholic drinks where your child can get to them. Liquor cabinets should have doors with safety latches or locks, and any liquor in the refrigerator should be stored in the back on the highest shelf. Make sure that there are no alcoholic drinks left out at night, since some children get up very early and can find and drink these leftover drinks. It does not take much alcohol to make your child very ill.
- If you use a diaper pail, make sure that it has a secure lid. Deodorant discs are poisonous and your child, after watching you put a new one in, may want to put it in her mouth.
- Always put the cap on, and tightly close the cap on a container of cleaning fluid or any other dangerous product whenever you put it down, even if it's only for a minute or if you are still using it.
- Do not take medicine or vitamins in front of your child or give her medicine and tell her it's candy. She will want to take it on her own.

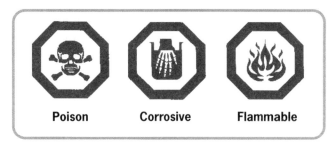

Water Safety

"My dad was the one who started us in the water. I don't know when we learned it, but I always think of water safety now—it's second nature."

Playing in the water is fun, and soothing, and can be a learning experience for your toddler. He may play in the bath, at the beach, in a wading pool, or with a bucket in the backyard. But whatever way your child plays in, on, or near the water, remember that, according to the Red Cross, drowning is one of the main causes of death in children between the ages of one and four. It's second only to car accidents.

You may think that, if you are in the general area when your child is in the water, he is safe enough.

Studies show that it only takes a moment when you are not looking for a child to drown.

Although there is risk with water play, there is also fun, exercise, and family time. Protect your toddler around any water. Keep your child safe by watching him at all times when you're around any water. Some parents buy a child-sized life jacket, checking the labels for the right size and weight, so they can relax a little bit, but they still watch their toddler carefully. Check your local community centre for toddler swim lessons. These are fun and will help to make your water time safer. Always hold onto a toddler's hand when on a dock or near a pool since it is common for a young child to suddenly run toward water. Be a good example and always wear a life jacket yourself when you are in any boat and put one on your toddler also.

"I had to work hard not to pass my fear of the water on to my daughter. I wanted her to like it, but still be really safe."

did you know?

Swimming pools, lakes, and the ocean are not the only water hazards. A child can drown in no more than 4 cm (1½ in.) of water, enough to cover his nose and mouth.

Follow these water-safety tips to make water play safer—but keep the pleasure.

Around the House and Yard

- *Never* leave your child in the bathtub when you are not there. Always stay in the room, right beside him.
- Teach the whole family to always put the lid down on the toilet seat and to keep the bathroom door closed. Curious toddlers can go head-first into a toilet and not be able to get out.
- Never leave a bucket of water near a toddler. It's easy to move on to another task when washing the floor—answering the phone, helping another child, or simply turning your back to pick something up. Your child can fall into the bucket and not be able to get her head out again.
- Lawn sprinklers that are left on too long can make puddles that are over 5 cm (2 in.) deep.

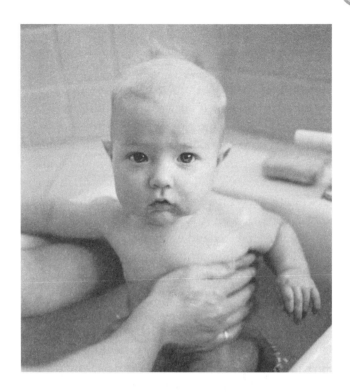

This is deep enough for a small child to slip in and be face-first in the water.

- Always empty your toddler's pool when it's not in use. Turn it upside down so that it doesn't collect rainwater.
- If you have a Jacuzzi or hot tub, be sure that the cover fits well and is in place whenever the tub isn't in use. Getting a lock for these covers is a very good idea. You must also be with a child of any age when in or near a Jacuzzi. If you are in a Jacuzzi or hot tub, the child must be no farther than one arm's length from you.

In Open Water or Pools

- You are the best life preserver possible for your child: *always be with and watch your child every moment that he's in a pool or near open water.* If you are leaving the area, even for a minute, take your child with you.
- Don't think that someone else is watching your children. If one person says that he or she will watch the children, be sure that person will watch ALL the time and can help a child if necessary.
- As early as possible, teach your children safe play at the pool. No running, no pushing, no diving, and *no swimming unless a careful adult is with them.*

- If you have a swimming pool, proper fencing is a must. There must also be a self-closing, spring-lock gate with a latch high enough that a child cannot reach it. An entrance to a pool through the house is a great hazard, and children must be watched even more closely in this situation.
- Never count on floatation devices such as water wings or air mattresses as a way to make your child safe—it is you who must make sure your child is safe. Floatation devices are not made to help children to be safe. Children can slip out or off them quickly and easily. You can make your toddler safer by putting an approved life jacket on him, but again, you must still watch him carefully all the time.
- Be sure there are no chairs, toys, tables, or other things that will help a toddler to climb into a fenced pool area or an above-ground pool.
- Empty your pool at the end of the season and cover it with an approved tarp. If the tarp fills with rainwater, drain it as soon as possible.
- Do not have any riding toys near the pool, since children can easily drive into the pool. Also, don't leave toys in the pool or open water where a child can see them and be interested in them. Instead, move the toys out to a safe area.
- Make sure that all chemicals for the pool are safely stored and locked away.

- Talk to your child about safety in boats and on docks. *"The water at the end of the dock is very deep, so you have to wear your life jacket at all times in case you fall in."* Hold onto your child when walking from one dock to another.
- If you are in a boat with your child, make sure that you are both wearing life jackets. Even if you can swim well, you need to be able to float so that you can help your child if your boat turns over.
- Talk with your child about what you are doing and why. Even when he may seem too young to understand what it is you are saying, he is listening to you and will slowly learn.
- If your child goes missing and there is any water source nearby, look for him there first.

Safety with Pets

Animals can be excellent friends for your child and your child can learn about what animals are like, how to be gentle, and how to care for them.

Tips on Pets and Children
- If you have a cat, keep the litter box in a place your child cannot get at. A young child will be very interested in a cat box and cat feces can contain harmful bacteria.
- If you have a sandbox, make sure that it has a lid so that pets and stray animals cannot use it as a litter box.

- Show your toddler how to be gentle when you handle your pet. Remember that your child will copy what she sees you doing at this stage.
- Never leave a young child on his own with a pet.
- Talk to her about how to act with animals. Teach her not to go to or pat an animal unless the owner says that this is okay. *"The dog likes to be patted gently; he doesn't like you to pull his tail or his ears. That hurts him and he may tell you to stop by barking or growling."*
- Explain that people should not take toys or bones away from a dog. Tell him not to touch an animal that is eating or sleeping. *"That's the puppy's special toy and he wants to chew on it now. He might try to bite you if you take it away from him."*
- If you are thinking of getting a pet, wait until your child is older, perhaps five or six. An older child will be able to understand your instructions and treat a pet with the care needed.
- If you have a pet, do not play in a rough way with it. Games such as tug of war on a rope, wrestling, or play biting can be dangerous if your pet tries to play them with your child.
- Never allow your pet to move freely in the house when your toddler is out of the crib or playpen.

did you know?

Children younger than five should not touch turtles or other reptiles, such as snakes or iguanas, or objects that touch these animals. Salmonella bacteria can make infants and toddlers very sick, and are often found on these animals.

Safety with Other People's Pets and Animals

- Always keep your child away from animals you do not know, and teach him not to go near an animal unless there is an adult around.
- Don't be shy about asking someone to put his dog on a leash. A child's safety comes before a dog's right to roam freely. Many parks have rules that dogs must be on a leash or well controlled.
- Always be with your child around animals, even ones you trust.

- When near a new mother cat or dog, do not go very close since they may feel threatened and bite or claw.
- If people visit with their dog, ask them to put the dog on a leash until your child has a chance to warm up to it, the dog becomes comfortable, and you have a chance to see if it is safe for the dog to be off the leash.

▶ **Q: "Since he was knocked down by a Lab in his early years, my son is terrified of dogs. What should we do?"**

▶ **A:** Being careful about an animal that is larger than you are is smart and should be encouraged. It is important to teach a child not to run when a dog is around even if he is afraid. To help your son feel more comfortable around dogs, ask a friend with a smaller, friendly, calm dog if you can visit with your child. Keep the dog on a leash and help your child just be in the same room at first. Later as your child shows you that he feels okay, you can put the dog on your lap while encouraging your child to be near. Alternately you can put your child on your lap and have your friend bring the dog over, which also gives him the advantage of being higher than the dog. While holding your child, talk with the dog, and have your child watch you pet the dog. The key is to slowly get closer and friendly with the dog. Let your child be in charge of the pace that he wants to go. Do not force your child to be with the dog, and, if he becomes upset, leave the room or have the dog go outside. It usually takes a very long time for fear to be easier to manage so change most certainly won't happen in one day. Be prepared for many visits. It helps if the visits can be with the same dog. Eventually your child may be prepared to pet the dog himself.

Go Play Outside!

Toddlers need fresh air and space where they can run and play, have fun, get dirty, and make noise. You need to be with them outdoors to share their fun, their energy, and to keep them safe.

The following are some points to think about and do to help your child to be safe outdoors.

In the Yard

- Are swimming pools or ponds fenced all the way around with self-closing safety gates?
- Is the playground equipment in good condition, well anchored, and the right size and height for your child's age?
- Is your yard fenced with a childproof safety latch on the gate?
- Is an adult with your child at all times when she is in the yard?
- Have poisonous plants been taken out?
- Is the ground surface under playground equipment made of wood chips, mulch, sand, or other recommended soft material?

In the Garage

- Is there an auto-reverse safety feature on the garage door so that it cannot crush your child? Does it work? (You can test whether it works by using a full paper towel roll.)
- Are sharp tools and power tools kept out of the reach of your child?
- Are chemicals that are used for gardens (fertilizer, pesticides) and automobiles (antifreeze) kept in a locked cabinet out of your child's reach?
- Are garbage and recycling containers closed or out of your child's reach?
- Is the garage, workshop, or garden shed locked up or does it have childproof handles?

Sun Protection

Protect your child from sunburns now so that the chance of skin cancer later in life is less. Your toddler has sensitive skin that is easily damaged by the sun, even on a cloudy or lightly overcast day. Here are some ideas to help protect your child:

- If your child is less than a year old, be sure to keep her out of direct sun. Put her under the shade of a tree or umbrella and dress her in light clothing. Stay with her if she is outside.
- Keep your toddler out of the sun between 10 a.m. and 4 p.m., when the sun's damaging rays are the most intense. If she must be out in the sun, dress her in a long-sleeved shirt, light long pants, and a broad-brimmed hat. Put sunscreen on unprotected areas.
- Do not wait for pink cheeks or skin to tell you that your child has had enough sun. Most sunburns won't really show the damage until six to 24 hours later. A severe burn will usually show up pink sooner.

> **Seek** shade. **Slip** on a shirt, **slap** on a hat, and **slop** on the sunscreen.

Sunscreen

Help your child put on sunscreen whenever she goes outside. Teach her what sunscreen is and why you're using it, in words she can understand. **Sunscreen and sun hats should fall into the same category as seat belts: "*We don't go out without them.*"** Again, think *monkey see, monkey do*—your toddler will usually happily copy what you do and make it a habit.

The best screens are rated at SPF 15 or higher. Choose sunscreens that are for children and approved by the Canadian Dermatology Association (look for their logo or name on the label). Lotion or milky, gel-like sunscreens may stay on the skin longer than sprays or oil-based ones.

Tips for Putting On Sunscreen

- First dab a test dose on a small area of your toddler's arm to see if she's sensitive to it.
- Sunscreen should cover **all** of your child's skin, including ears, nose, feet, the backs of knees, neck, and lips. (Check the labels. Regular sunscreen is not for lips, but you can get sunscreens made for lips that is safe.) It takes about one tablespoon to cover the entire skin surface of an average-sized toddler, so use a good amount. Be careful around the eyes, since sunscreen should not go in the eye. It will sting.
- For best effect, put sunscreen on 15 to 30 minutes before going outside, so it can be absorbed. (Some are absorbed very fast—check the label.)
- Sunscreens should be put on again, every two hours, depending on water exposure, wind, sweating, and rubbing with towels. (The product label will show how often to put it on.)
- If your child is playing in water, use a waterproof sunscreen and put it on again every couple of hours to make sure her skin will not burn.

Clothing

Clothing that helps protect from the sun may be easier for you and your child to manage than using sunscreen that can wash off. All materials provide some sun protection, but some materials can help protect better than others do. Those materials that protect better are very heavy fabrics with a tight weave. White fabrics may give more protection than off-white because they reflect the sun's rays better; dark fabric protects better than white does. Fabrics that have shrunk so that the weave is tighter may also give more protection. More information on fabrics that protect better is coming from places like Australia. Some children's summer outfits are now being made so that they have a higher UV protection factor, are quick-drying, and lightweight.

For best protection, dress your child in loose, darker coloured clothes with a tighter weave. It's best if the clothes have been washed, but are not too worn. Your child should put on a comfortable hat with a large brim and neck cover, and put sunscreen on any skin not covered by clothing. Remember to remove hood strings or neck strings from toddler clothes to prevent strangulation.

Clothing that does not protect very well is made of very lightweight fabrics with an open weave, such as light woven cottons, stretched fabrics or older, worn clothing.

Sunglasses

Your toddler's eyes can be damaged by the sun's ultraviolet rays, so protect them with sunglasses or clear plastic glasses. Make sure the sunglasses have a label that says they give full protection from UV radiation. If your child does not want to wear sunglasses, try the clear plastic glasses that have been tested for UV blocking or buy a wide-brimmed hat that has a big enough brim to protect his eyes. Make sure he puts it on whenever he's outside. Even better is a hat with a flap at the back to protect his neck as well.

Sunglasses should:

- Have lenses that fully cover the eyes.
- Fit well and be comfortable for your child.
- Have a wraparound design that protects the side of the eye.

On very hot or humid days, the body's natural cooling system needs more water so it can work well. Heat can build up in the body and may result in *heat exhaustion* or heatstroke.

Make sure that your toddler drinks fluids regularly when he's outdoors in the heat, that he has time to cool off out of the sun, and that he has the right clothes on for the weather. Carry a water bottle with you and give your child a drink every hour or so. Never leave children in a hot car by themselves, not even for a minute!

Symptoms of heat exhaustion are fatigue, weakness, confusion, nausea, headache, muscle cramps, and pale, clammy skin. Heat exhaustion is usually not life-threatening, but it is best to take the time to plan so this does not happen.

If your child has these symptoms, bring him indoors or into the shade, loosen or remove his clothing, give him a bath in cool water, and encourage him to drink water. *Consult your doctor if your child continues to show signs of heat exhaustion or is vomiting.*

Hats for Sun Protection

Hats may be one of your best friends when it comes to sun protection. Hats can protect most of the face and eyes, and some will also protect the neck. And they are often easier to keep on a child than sunglasses are. Make sure the hat fits well and your child likes it. A hat that is too small will fall off or be pulled off, and a hat that is too large can slip down over his eyes and will be pulled off, or make walking hard. For the best sun protection, look for hats with a wide brim, "French foreign legion" hats, or hats with a back-of-the-neck flap. Most hats for young children do not have ties or neck elastic because they can be dangerous if they are tangled around the neck; also, they are often not very comfortable. A hat that fits well should not need ties and will pull on over the head well enough that it will not come off easily.

Winter Weather

Playing outdoors in the winter can be fun, but it is not safe in extremely cold weather. Keep your child indoors any time the temperature (including the wind chill factor) falls below -28°C.

For safe winter play, dress your toddler in warm layers and make sure he comes in often to get warm, usually about every 30 minutes. If you and your toddler need to be out in very cold weather for any length of time, look for signs of frostnip, the early warning signal for frostbite.

Frostnip is whiteness and numbness on the cheeks, nose, ears, fingers, or toes. If your child has frostnip:

- Bring him indoors immediately.
- Remove wet clothing. (It takes heat away from the body.)

- Immerse chilled body parts in warm water. Generally, once the feeling comes back, you can stop; however, a young child may not be able to tell you this so you will need to watch his behaviour. Make sure you know that the water is just warm because your child won't feel the heat if his hands are numb, and he could be burned if the water is too hot.

did you know?

 Children lose heat from their skin faster than adults do, so they're at greater risk for frostbite.

Safety in the Community

Streetproofing

Awareness and a certain amount of worry are healthy and useful in keeping parents alert and aware of their children's whereabouts and safety. The topic of safety and streetproofing is often a scary one for parents. You want to help your toddler begin to develop self-protection skills and caution, but not to be afraid.

Streetproofing is helping your child to develop and use good sense in traffic, in any abuse situation, or if she is lost. Knowing what to do and doing it (self-confidence) is something you can teach your child to help her make safe decisions. Encourage your child to talk to you about anything—or anyone—that makes her uncomfortable, from an early age. See page 13 for more information on sexual development of your toddler and words you can use to describe her body parts.

Check with Me First

Children, and many adults, find great pleasure in talking with each other and in giving small gifts and treats. With your support, being around people that your child doesn't know can be a positive experience for all. Learning trust in her environment and community is a part of normal development. One way of keeping safety in mind and helping your child to learn about her world is to teach the "Check with

me first" approach. She must check with you or her caregiver first before going anywhere with anyone, or taking a gift or treats. *"Before you go anywhere with anyone, check with me first, even if it's with your Aunt Cindy."* The focus of your teaching is that *"I need to know where you are all the time, and what things are given to you. Then we both know that you are safe."* Let other caregivers know that you use this system so that they can do the same thing and teach your child about safety the same way you do.

Children learn by watching and following their parents and caregivers. So talk as you do things—this is a good way to teach and practise any kind of safe behaviour. Look both ways before you cross a street with your child, for example, and make it a habit to point out what you are doing: *"We're carefully looking both ways first—see the car?" "We won't run out here because there may be a car coming—let's look for a crosswalk or clear spot first." "What do we all do when we get in the car? Buckle up."* Be very clear in your communication. Saying, *"Be careful on the tricycle,"* will not help your toddler to understand and take action, but *"Look up the driveway when you ride"* or *"You must wear your helmet when you're on your bike"* will help.

Keep instructions simple. Start off with what must be followed and talk about the reasons in a simple way. It will help your child to learn more quickly if you use the same words and ideas over and over. Also, your actions should be the same as your instructions—you always walk in a crosswalk to cross the street when going to the store, even if it means walking half a block more.

The "What If" Game

Three-year-old children can usually say their name and may even be able to repeat their address. Practise this with your child by playing the "What If" game with her. *"What if I were a police officer and you were lost? What would you tell me?" "What if you didn't know me and I wanted you to come with me? What would you do?"*

Showing your child what she can do and what not to do helps her to develop a safety zone or boundaries. A toddler does not yet have the ability to make good decisions and may forget what she learned yesterday. Even though you are going to stay in the yard with your child, teach her about her limits. Don't just say, *"We are going to stay in the yard"*; instead, walk with her around the yard and show her how far she can go. *"You can't go past the big tree, but you can play anywhere in front of it."*

Young children are trying to understand the ideas of movement, climbing, and speaking, and can easily run off to something because they are interested. They are not going to be able to be street smart. Keeping them safe is up to parents or caregivers. A natural shyness and fear of strangers may make most children scream or cry if a stranger picks them up, but this is not always the case.

Sadly, statistics show that most sexual abuse of children is by someone they know and trust. Think about and be sure you are comfortable with whomever you leave your child with, and think about who else may be around your child while she is in someone else's care. Encourage your child to tell you if she is not comfortable with any adult she is around or who cares for her. This means that as a parent you must listen carefully to your child and encourage her concerns, especially about friends and relatives.

Could Someone Take My Child?

The vast majority of abductions in Canada are by the child's own parent. Many of these cases are resolved quickly, but they still cause great stress and fear. If you are in or have left a difficult relationship, keep a recent picture of your child and his parent, and a current list of the telephone number and addresses of your ex-partner's family and friends. As well, keep on record the make and year of his or her car and licence plate number. You may never need this information, but in the event of an abduction, the police can work faster if they have this information quickly. Some communities have child identification events where you can have a picture taken and fingerprints done for you to keep. Many parents go to these events so that they have a record, even when they do not have immediate concerns. Many communities also have block parent programs that you may want to know more about or be part of. (See page 118 for further information.)

Safety on the Move

Strollers

Strollers make it easier for you and your child to enjoy being out, shopping, or just walking together. When you buy a stroller, think about where you want to go and how you will use it. If you live in a community where you are near the stores and the shopping you need, then you may want a big stroller

that can carry shopping bags. Maybe you need a stroller that fits into your car or one that you can easily take on the bus. Some jogging strollers that have larger wheels and seat may be too big for your car and cannot go on a bus easily, but are more comfortable for you and your toddler when you're out in the community. An umbrella or folding type may be more useful. Make sure that the stroller you buy has a good security strap and use it all the time.

How to Avoid Injuries
- Choose a sturdy stroller that is recommended for your child's weight and height.
- Always use the security straps to prevent your child from falling forward, tipping the stroller over, or setting it in motion.
- Watch out for fingers when you're folding or unfolding the stroller and when you're reversing the handle.
- Use the brake at all times if the stroller is standing still, and never leave your child alone in a stroller. Many children are injured when left in strollers on their own.
- Pay attention to the balance of the stroller when you are carrying heavy packages. A backpack may be better for carrying these items or you may need to make two trips.
- Check the stroller regularly for sharp edges, tears in the upholstery, brakes that don't work, or loose wheels.
- Check older models to make sure they won't fold up when your child is in them.

Back Carriers

Back carriers help you to walk with your child with your hands free, and do not require a flat or even surface as a stroller does.

Look for a carrier that:
- Has a safety strap and use it all the time.
- Has leg openings that are small enough to keep your child from slipping out, but large enough that they will not rub on your child's legs.
- Is quite light but well made.
- Has a folding frame that won't pinch your child.
- Has a padded covering over the metal frame near your child's face.

Bicycle Trailers and Seats

Wait until your toddler is about 12 months old for her first ride in a bicycle-mounted trailer, child seat, sidecar, or any other carrier. Even a slow, careful bike ride causes plenty of jolts and shocks for a tiny body. If possible, try to ride on multi-use paths since they are safer, quieter, and the air is often better than on a roadway. Before taking your toddler in any carrier, practise turning, stopping, and hill climbing with a bag of flour or other weight so you can feel and learn how to manage the extra load. When a child is in a trailer or bike seat, **put an approved bicycle helmet on her and do up the safety belt.**

Learn about "Bike Smarts" for children. This manual is available from the Insurance Corporation of British Columbia (ICBC) and on line at www.icbc.com/communities/bikesmarts.pdf

Helmets
- Helmets are needed—all children must wear them if riding in a trailer or bike seat.
- The neck development of a one-year-old may not support the weight of a helmet. If in doubt, take the helmet and your toddler to your family doctor and ask.
- Approved bicycle safety helmets have a CSA, ANSI, ASTM, or SNELL standard clearly marked.
- Choose a round helmet rather than one that is "aero" shaped, since the tail will hit the back of the seat and force the child's head forward.
- If using a trailer, provide a cushion to support your toddler's head when your child goes to sleep.

Trailers

- Trailers usually cost twice as much as child seats, and they protect your toddler better if you fall. A very young child may not be safe in a trailer. Talk to the dealer and read the manufacturer's instructions.
- Trailers can be used for one or two children of up to 45 kilograms (100 pounds) total weight. Toddlers often find their "tents on wheels" a good place to nap or play with their toys, so have soft toys and a pillow on board.
- Use a bike flag so the cars can see you well. Usually you will be out only in the daytime or in good weather with a toddler, but if you are out at night or in bad weather, make sure the trailer has a tail light and reflector.

Bicycle-Mounted Child Seats

- Seats are for children who are over one year and up to 18 kilograms (40 pounds) in weight. They are not for very young children.
- Choose a rear-wheel-mounted seat with spoke protectors and have it put on by an experienced person at the bicycle shop.
- Check that the child's feet, hands, and clothing are well away from the spokes or other moving parts of the bike.

- Expect to be put off-balance when your child moves suddenly.
- Never leave a child alone in this carrier.

Car Safety

The two most important keys to protecting your child in the car are: make sure he is safely buckled into the child seat, and be well aware of the road and other cars when driving (drive defensively).

Car and truck crashes kill more than 70 children under the age of five and injure another 4000 children every year in Canada. Make sure that your child seat is correctly installed (see below for correct installation) and use only approved child seats that meet the Canadian Motor Vehicle Safety Standards (CMVSS). Child safety seats must be used by law in British Columbia.

Child Safety Seats

As your child grows, she will move from an infant seat (Stage 1) to a convertible seat (Stage 2). Your child can then move into a combination/harness booster seat when older than about three years old.

The transition from an infant seat to a convertible seat is when the child reaches at least one year of age and 10 kilograms (22 pounds) in weight. Do not move your child to the next step too soon.

Stage 1–Infant Seats (Rear Facing)

Children less than 12 months of age are transported in a car in a rear-facing position. This is because in a crash the weak neck ligaments and soft neck bones in infants younger than 12 months old would not protect the spinal cord, and severe injuries can occur. When riding facing the rear, the head and neck are supported and move together with the body, providing better protection. In a crash, the back of the rear-facing infant seat takes the force of the impact instead of the child's neck.

- Infant seats must always be used in the rear-facing position. The safest place to install the infant seat is in the middle of the car's back seat.
- Infant seats are held in place by your car's seat belt. Refer to the car's instruction manual for details on how your seat is best secured.
- If your child outgrows the infant seat (that is, if he weighs over 10 kilograms or 22 pounds) and is still under one year of age, move him to a convertible seat, but keep him rear-facing until he reaches one year of age.

- **Never place an infant restraint in a front seat equipped with air bags. Serious injury or death may result if an air bag inflates and strikes a rear-facing child seat.**

> Before moving your child from an infant seat to a convertible seat, make sure she meets the weight requirements.

Stage 2–Convertible Seats

These seats are called "convertible" because they can be used in rear-facing or forward-facing positions.

Rear-facing convertible seats:
- Rear-facing convertible seats are held in place with your car's seat belt.
- A convertible seat should be used only when your child has outgrown the infant seat. Use the convertible seat in the rear-facing position until your child is at least one year of age.
- Many convertible seats indicate that they can be used forward-facing when the child is over 9 to 10 kilograms (20 to 22 pounds). However, it is much safer to keep your child in a rear-facing position for as long as possible.
- Some rear-facing convertible seats are suitable for infants up to 16 kilograms (35 pounds).

Forward-facing convertible seats:
- All forward-facing convertible seats that are approved by CMVSS will have a tether strap located on the back of the safety seat.
- In addition to holding the seat in place with a regular seat belt, the tether strap must be anchored to the vehicle's frame to prevent the seat from pitching forward or to the side in a crash. Cars built after 1989 (with the exception of convertibles) have a predrilled and threaded anchorage slot. Check the vehicle's owner manual for installation instructions.
- If you are unsure if your vehicle has an anchorage slot, or if it is not a passenger car, take the vehicle to your dealership for information and assistance.
- Most forward-facing convertible seats are suitable for a child weighing up to 18 kilograms (40 pounds).

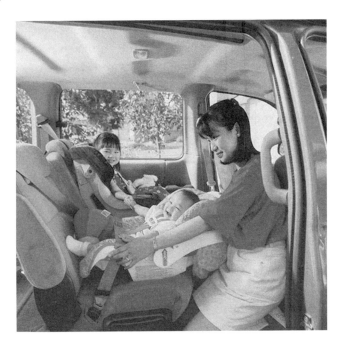

With both the infant and convertible restraint systems, make sure that:

- The seat carries a CMVSS label indicating that it meets Canadian Motor Vehicle Safety Standards.
- You have read the manufacturer's instructions and have installed the seat properly.
- The car seat is placed in the middle of the back seat. **Never place any restraint in the front seat of a car equipped with an air bag system.**
- The shoulder harness is adjusted to allow no more than a finger-width space between the harness and your child's body. The straps should not be twisted.
- Your child is not bundled in blankets or a bunting bag under the harness straps, as this will interfere with a proper fit. Place blankets on top of your child only after he is buckled into the seat. Dress your child so that the buckle can latch between his legs.
- If there is a chest clip to hold the harness straps in position, it should be raised to the level of your child's armpits.
- The harness straps pass through the slots in the back of the child seat so that they are level with your child's shoulders or slightly above. Almost all child seats can use the top set of harness slots only when in the forward-facing position. Make sure to check your child seat manual.

- The restraint fits on the seat of your vehicle and, if it is a forward-facing seat, it is secured to your vehicle using tether anchorage hardware.
- Every time you put your child in the car, check that the child seat does not move from side to side or forward and back more than 2.5 cm (1 inch) when you pull on it.
- The child seat is less than 10 years old and has not passed the expiry date recommended by the manufacturer.
- You do not leave your child sleeping unsupervised in the car seat in your home or car.

Used Child Seats

If you are buying a secondhand child seat, make sure it meets all CMVS standards. Do not place your child in a used infant, convertible, or booster seat if:

- The seat is on a recall list.
- The harness straps or padded liner is frayed, torn, or detached from the seat.
- There are any cracks in the plastic shell.
- The tubular frame is bent or rusted at the rivet points.
- The seat is older than 10 years or past the manufacturer's expiry date.
- The CMVSS label is not attached or the manufacturer's instructions are missing.
- The tether strap or tether anchorage is frayed, torn, or missing (convertible seat only).
- The child seat does not fit properly into your car. Not all child seats fit properly into every car. Before you buy one, check to make sure it fits into your car securely.
- You are unsure of the child seat's history. Note that some crashes may damage a child seat (even damage from a serious crash may be hard to see).

The use of an infant seat is one of the most important points in car safety, but it is not the only rule to follow. Remember:

- The safest seat in the car is in the middle of the back seat, so whenever possible, place your child's seat there. All children under 12 should be secured in the back seat for the best safety.
- Always buckle your toddler into his child seat no matter how short the trip, and check occasionally that he's still in his seat.

- If you have no alternative but to transport your child in the front seat, deactivate the air bag, put the seat back as far as it will go, and properly secure your child. Be aware of side air bags and keep your child away from them.
- Always keep your child seat secured with the seat belt, even if it's not in use. Keep other loose objects, such as anti-theft clubs, under the seat as they can become fatal missiles in a crash.
- If you have a station wagon or sport utility and transport a pet, use a removable metal partition and put your pet in the back. This stops your pet from being thrown into passengers in a crash and also reduces distractions while you are driving.
- If you need to use a cellular phone in the car, pull over first, and then make your call.
- Allowing your children to play with the power windows is unsafe. If you as the driver have the controls, keep them locked. Always check that fingers, heads, and arms are inside the car before you adjust the windows yourself.
- If you are having an argument with your child, or find that you are very distracted by him, pull over until you have the situation under control. It is not safe to drive while your focus is on your child.
- Regularly check your car for, and remove, objects such as small balls or toys that can easily be dropped in the back seat and roll forward until they are under the brake pedal.
- Children should not play in or near a parked car. A toddler can easily release a brake or take a car out of gear.

For more information on child seats, contact your nearest ICBC office, or call Safe Start (listed in the reference section).

▶ **Q: "A lap belt works for us, so why not a child too?"**
▶ **A:** When looking at your lap belt, you will notice that it is designed to pass over your pelvic bone and that the shoulder belt passes over your chest. Both are large bony structures that protect the soft organs inside. Because children are so much smaller than adults, lap belts fit over their soft abdomens, not their bony structures. Even if a child isn't thrown from the car in a crash, he can be severely injured by having his internal organs damaged by the belt itself.

▶ **Q: "I'm sitting right beside her and holding on. Does she really need a restraint?"**
▶ **A:** We would like to think we can protect our children from all dangers, but most crashes are so sudden and violent that you would not be able to hold on to your child at all.

A Guide to Further Resources

ALCOHOL AND DRUG INFORMATION

All provinces and territories have programs for people with alcohol and other drug problems. Ask your doctor or public health nurse for assistance or check in the yellow pages of your telephone book under "Alcohol" or "Drug" information. You can also call the **Alcohol and Drug Information and Referral line** at 1-800-663-1441. This line is confidential and toll-free and offers information about drug and alcohol programs in the Province of BC. Local program information is also available through your Native Friendship Centres.

There are programs available for smokers who would like help to quit the habit. Contact your local public health unit, Canadian Cancer Society, or local lung association for information on programs near you.

BLOCK PARENT PROGRAMS

The Block Parent Program of Canada was incorporated in 1986 and now has registered committees in most provinces and territories. Block Parents are volunteer adults who offer refuge and assistance to children in times of emergency. All volunteers are screened by the police and have received program training. For more information, contact the BC Block Parent Society at 250-474-2494.

CAR SEATS

Your public health unit or community agencies such as recreation centres will have information regarding rental services of car seats.

For information on child restraints, call **Transport Canada** at 1-800-333-0371 or contact your local ICBC office. The number will be in the white pages of your telephone directory. Residents of BC can also contact ICBC by writing to: Public Affairs and Corporate Marketing, **Insurance Corporation of British Columbia**, 240 – 151 West Esplanade, North Vancouver, BC, V7M 3H9. Or visit their Web site at www.icbc.com

CHILD CARE

For more information on selecting a child-care facility, contact the **Child Care Resource and Referral Program** (CCRR). To find out if there is a CCRR in your area, you can call the Enquiry BC number in the blue pages of your phone book, or toll free at 1-800-663-7867. For more information about child care: www.mcaws.gov.bc.ca

You can contact the local licensing program in your health region for a copy of the booklet entitled **A Parent's Guide to Selecting Child Care**. If you need help in contacting the licensing program in your health region, contact Enquiry BC, toll-free at 1-800-663-7867, or in Vancouver at 604-660-2421. This booklet is also available on the Web at: www.healthplanning.gov.bc.ca

For information about applying for child-care subsidy, contact your local Ministry of Community, Aboriginal and Women's Services office through the Enquiry BC number.

CHILDREN WITH DISABILITIES

There are services available if your child has developmental problems or a disability. Your doctor, public health nurse, or social services office can help you locate these services. Many communities have an Infant Development Program for children from birth to age three. Staff in this program may assist you in providing activities for your child that will encourage his or her development, and in accessing other supports that may help you and your child. A diagnosis of a developmental problem for a young child is difficult for any parent, but there are many other parents and professionals to help you at this time and as your child grows older. A child with severe disabilities may be eligible for the benefits of the At Home Program, which is available through Ministry of Children and Family Development.

FAMILY VIOLENCE

If you are concerned about, or dealing with violence or threatened violence, contact your local office of the **Ministry of Community, Aboriginal and Women's Services** (see the blue pages in the telephone directory under Province of BC). You can also call the women's helpline or transition house listed in the front page of your telephone directory or in the white pages. If you or your children are in danger, do not hesitate to call the police.

FIRST AID

For emergency numbers such as the police, fire, ambulance, and poison information centre, look inside the front page of your telephone book.

The **Canadian Red Cross Society** offers a "Childsafe Program" that teaches CPR and basic skills for dealing with emergencies. For more information, contact your local branch of the Red Cross listed in the white pages of your telephone book or call toll-free 1-888-307-7997.

St. John Ambulance offers programs in first aid, CPR, and child care. You can find the number for your local branch of St. John Ambulance in the white pages of the telephone directory or in the yellow pages under "First Aid Services."

HEALTH RESOURCE

The **BC HealthGuide Program** has three components to give you high quality health information to help you manage any health care condition or concern for you and your family, any time of the day or night.

The **BC HealthGuide Handbook** has BC specific information on over 190 health concerns including prevention, symptoms, emergencies, home treatment, when to call a health professional, and BC resources. To request a copy, call **1-800-465-4911**.

The **BC HealthGuide OnLine** (bchealthguide.org) links you to a world of reliable and up-to-date health information, including BC specific information and links to other web-sites, plus access to the Healthwise Knowledgebase that contains a vast library of health information with over 2,500 easy-to-read health topics.

The **BC HealthGuide NurseLine** operates 24 hours a day, seven days a week and puts you in touch with specially trained Registered Nurses who can answer your questions about any health condition or concern, to help you make better health care decisions for you and your family. Translation services are available upon request in 130 languages.
Local calling in Greater Vancouver: **604-215-4700**
Toll-free elsewhere in BC: **1-866-215-4700**
Deaf and hearing-impaired toll-free in BC: **1-866-TTY-4700**

The **BC HealthGuide Program** complies with the Freedom of Information and Protection of Privacy Act and collects your personal information only when necessary to provide you with the specific service you request.

NUTRITION

You can get a copy of *Canada's Food Guide to Healthy Eating* on line at www.hc-sc.gc.ca/hppb/nutrition/pube/foodguid/foodguide.html or from your health unit.

You can also talk with a dietitian on a toll-free nutrition and food safety line at 1-800-667-3438 (Dial-a-Dietitian).

PARENTING

"Nobody's Perfect" is a no-cost educational program for parents of children under age five. It meets the needs of young, single, low-income, socially or geographically isolated parents or parents with limited formal education. (It is not intended for families in crisis or those with serious problems.) You can find out about programs offered in your community by contacting your local public health unit, Prenatal Outreach Program (POP), Native Friendship Centre, or local recreation centre.

Also talk with your public health nurse or agencies such as a community recreation centre about other parenting programs that may be offered in your community.

For information about enforcement of maintenance orders, contact the Family Maintenance Enforcement Program in the blue pages of your telephone book or call toll-free 1-800-663-3455.

POSTPARTUM DEPRESSION

Your doctor or public health unit are good sources of information about local postpartum support groups and programs.

The **Pacific Post Partum Support Society** has a guide for mothers who are experiencing postpartum depression entitled *Post Partum Depressions and Anxiety, A Self-Help Guide for Mothers*. For information about local postpartum depression support groups, contact your public health nurse or the Society at: Pacific Post Partum Support Society, # 104 – 1416 Commercial Drive, Vancouver, BC. V5L 3X9 or on-line at: pppss@postpartum.org

SAFE START

Safe Start is an injury-prevention program of BC's Children's Hospital. It provides information to parents and caregivers on how to make homes and cars safer. For more information from within BC, call 1-888-331-8100.

Index